PHANTOM SIGNS

ALSO BY PHILIP BRADY

POETRY

Forged Correspondences (New Myths, 1996)
Weal (Ashland Poetry Press, 1999)
Fathom (WordTech, 2007)
To Banquet with the Ethiopians: A Memoir of Life Before the Alphabet
    (Broadstone, 2015)

PROSE

To Prove My Blood: A Tale of Emigrations & the Afterlife (Ashland, 2004)
By Heart: Reflections of a Rust Belt Bard (University of Tennessee, 2008)

EDITED COLLECTIONS

Essays on Joyce's Portrait (Twayne, 1998)
Poems and Their Making: A Conversation (Etruscan, 2015)

1/18/2020

PHANTOM SIGNS

THE
MUSE
IN
UNIVERSE
CITY

PHILIP BRADY

THE UNIVERSITY OF TENNESSEE PRESS / KNOXVILLE

LIBRARY OF CONGRESS CATALOGING-IN-PUBLICATION DATA

Names: Brady, Philip, 1955– author.

Title: Phantom signs : the muse in Universe City / Philip Brady.

Description: First edition. | Knoxville : The University of Tennessee Press, [2018] |

Identifiers: LCCN 2018043541 (print) | LCCN 2018059191 (ebook) |

ISBN 9781621904700 (pdf) | ISBN 9781621904717 (kindle) |

ISBN 9781621904694 (paperback)

Subjects: LCSH: Brady, Philip, 1955- | Authors, American—21st century—
Biography. | Poets, American—21st century—Biography. |
Publishers and publishing—United States—Biography.

Classification: LCC PS3552.R2437 (ebook) | LCC PS3552.R2437 Z46 2018 (print) |
DDC 814/.54—dc23

LC record available at https://lccn.loc.gov/2018043541

FOR ELSA

MY BEAUTIFUL HUMAN WIFE WAS BORN A SELKIE

CONTENTS

ACKNOWLEDGMENTS

"Basketball at 60" first appeared on the Best American Poetry blog.

"Face" first appeared in *The Green Mountain Review*.

"The Man of Double Deed" and "English" were first published in *Hotel Amerika*.

"*Authenticité*" appeared in *By Heart: Reflections of a Rust Belt Bard* (Univ. of Tennessee Press, 2008).

"Jack" was first published in *A Slant of Light: Festschrift for Jack Wheatcroft* (Bucknell Univ. Press, 2018).

"Commencement" was delivered to the Wilkes University MFA Class of 2016 in Mesa, Arizona.

Translations from the *Iliad* and the *Odyssey* are from Ian Johnston's web page, "Johnstonia." Translations of Roberto Manzano are by Steven Reese, from *Synergos: Selected Poems of Roberto Manzano* (Etruscan Press, 2011). "Strawberry" by Paisley Rekdal was published in *The Invention of the Kaleidoscope* (University of Pittsburgh, 2007).

I am deeply indebted to friends and colleagues who have commented on and encouraged this book: J. Michael Lennon, Lynn Lurie, Gary McDowell, Kevin Oderman, Robert Mooney, and Sam Pickering. Thank you Janine Dubik, Jeannie Saoirse , and Karley Stasko for their close reading and to Aurora Bonner and Bill Schneider for all their help. Deep gratitude for shared laughter, sharp insight, and uplifting support from colleagues and students in the Wilkes University Creative Writing Program and from its stalwart leader, Bonnie Culver, and thanks to Youngstown State University for a research professorship which gave me time to complete this book. Finally, deep gratitude and respect for Scot Danforth at UT Press, who stood by this book, saw it through, and never faltered.

INTRODUCTION

"One of the most startling paradoxes inherent in writing," says Walter Ong, "is its close association with death." *Phantom Signs* explores this paradox from dual perspectives: I am a writer. I am also a publisher.

This book emerges from the tension between these modes of being in the world: the writer's dark; the editor's light. Each faces the presence of death—the substitution of the written word for living breath. Each faces questions of identity—as one essay "Nothing Attested, Everything Sung" humorously mixes up the author with one of the writers he publishes.

The essays address another paradox—the way we apprehend the world through two species of language: written word and spoken utterance. The written word is recorded and is outside the temporal. Utterance depends on time and place and breath; it is immediate, ephemeral, and malleable. Poetry began as utterance and flourished a very long time before its transliteration into the written word. As a writer and publisher, I experience poetry as utterance, as word, as history, and as commercial and aesthetic artifact. This experience is primarily located in "Universe City"—that is, academia—a space that contends with and shapes these channels.

The perspectives of these essays intersect. With forty years at Universe Cities in America, Ireland, and Africa, I have experienced ways in which nontraditional students negotiate oral and written language. For instance, the essay "The Man of Double Deed" describes an exercise I have done many times in unlikely venues—third grade classes, bars, graduate seminars, hedge-fund offices, and campsites. I recite a poem of fourteen lines one time, and the audience learns it by heart, demonstrating the power of the aural imagination. As a publisher of an independent, nonprofit literary press, I am engaged in the aesthetic and commercial aspects of contemporary letters, and in the first essay, "The Book I Almost Wrote," I discuss poetry from the point of view of the publisher/editor. Another essay, "Face," spins out of the recent disturbing conviction of Kirk Nesset, a professor of creative writing at Allegheny College, on charges of child pornography. The essay delves into the ways that reportage constructs our response to the world. As a former basketball player, I bring attention to bear on the way age alters the body and mind in "Basketball at 60." And as the director of a Poetry Center, hosting hundreds of readings, I discuss the pros and cons of the poetry reading circuit in an essay called "That Lamp Is From the Tomb." Two essays, "Kith and Kin" and "Are Lives Matter?" explore identity as it relates to race, while another, "Edited," explores identity after death.

Finally, the essay from which the book takes its title, "Nine Phantom Signs," emerges from a life event and its results. In 2010, at the age of fifty-five, I felt shortness of breath while doing laps in a pool. The next day I was wheeled into St. Elizabeth's hospital in Youngstown, Ohio, for coronary triple bypass surgery. I spent the months of recovery mulling over a long prose memoir I had been working on, *To Banquet with the Worthy Ethiopians: A Memoir of Life Before the Alphabet*. The memoir begins in an office in "Universe City," where an aging writer broods on a list which he keeps folded in a copy of the *Iliad*. Item 265 reads simply "Thersites," a foot soldier whining to go home. The writer recalls the summer he first encountered the *Iliad*. Though overwhelmed by the turgid prose, he gleans enough to realize that the Trojan War, with all its violence and intrigue, was being waged on a smaller scale at his summer camp.

In the dreamy state following the surgery, the events of half a century ago seemed foreign, distant, and walled off by sentences. Why reconstruct details from so long ago? Instead, I began to transcribe the prose into blank verse, hearing cadences that seemed close and ephemeral as the breath I'd nearly lost. *To Banquet with the Ethiopians: A Memoir of Life Before the Alphabet*, a book-length poem of eighteen chapters, was published in 2015 by Broadstone Books. In many ways, *Phantom Signs* has come out of the experience of turning sentences into lines and back again into sentences.

So much, of course, has been written about poetry. What is it? Who owns it? Is it dead? But most criticism shares one assumption: poetry is a genre. It can be identified and judged on the page, or, if not there, then in performance. *Phantom Signs* calls that assumption into question. I say that poetry is not a genre like fiction or creative nonfiction or screenwriting or playwriting. Poetry is, as I argue in one essay, "nought." It manifests as a human faculty, rather than the result of human effort. It is not addressed to the human community (and still less to God or any of his minions). It is the impression left upon the mind when all writing has been effaced.

Despite being a publisher, I hope I don't sound like a Poetry Salesman. I don't know if poetry can be enjoyed by everyone. I do know that poetry is immersed in "everything that happens and does not." May these Phantom Signs reveal nought. And may they sell (can't help meself). Have at it. Dive in.

WE THE UNDERSIGNED

wish to express our collective outrage at the usage of our names, monikers, aliases, titles, and appurtenances without notice or permission in the text called *Phantom Signs: The Muse in Universe City*. While we represent widely diverse occupations, origins, and existential conditions—comprising members of the mortal, immortal, mythical, fairy tale, fictional, animal, and animation communities, we stand united in our disavowal of this gross act of appropriation.

We are, we attest, more than "Phantom Signs." Alive, deceased, or neither, our imaginations are free and rampant, and we protest this reduction from autonomous beings to chirographic symbols drawn by an unauthorized person. Many of the characteristics attributed to us in this text are distorted, and numerous statements made about us or on our behalf are, we believe, libelous.

While the vast majority of the undersigned have never met the author and cannot speak to his status as publisher, writer, and musician, he himself writes of his nonprofit literary press that "few buy and fewer follow." His own publisher, who is among the undersigned, grants that the author's latest release, *To Banquet with the Ethiopians: A Memoir of Life Before the Alphabet* (more anon) has never cracked the Small Press Distribution best-seller list, despite elegant production in cloth and paper editions and assiduous marketing. As for his music, the undersigned who have heard him perform—including his fellow band members and his wife—concur that he sings off key, fakes a brogue, and fudges lyrics. Sound techs routinely mute his bodhrán mic. His tin whistle, reports his cat Molly (see undersigned), is terrifying.

Even the author's claim to Irish heritage is bogus. While it is true that he grew up in a time when his native Queens was virtually the thirty-third county, DNA analysis has revealed that prominent strands of his ancestry derive from far-flung locales including Beantown, Berkeley, Brigadoon, Chelsea, Christiansted, Flatbush, Guadalajara, Hawaii, Hisarlik, Mordor, Motherwell, Ogygia, Owego, Petropavlovsk, La Rue de la Honte, Shinbone, Waterbury, and Zaire. Conspicuously absent is Ethiopia.

Phantom Signs is rife with dubious claims, fake news, jaundiced insinuation, and factual error. To list just a few:

1. The incessant rocking and chanting referenced to invoke trance, poetic rhythms, and/or communion with the Muse (more anon) is in fact likely symptomatic of some neurological disorder. According to an affidavit from the author's brother, who is not among the undersigned but has acted as "friend of the court" throughout our proceedings, these antic fits branded the author as a social misfit from an early age.

2. The distinguished chair of our antiquities committee, Melesigines (aka Homer), testifies that while claims of the bard's birthplace range from Greece to Troy to Cambridgeshire to Spain, no sightings have ever been credibly verified in Queens, despite multiple allusions in *Phantom Signs* and several chapters in *To Banquet with the Ethiopians* devoted to wholly fantastical events including but not limited to a tavern workshop in which the *Iliad* is savaged by a pride of all-star nudniks, a sexual encounter with the Muse in a scene (Nighttown) pirated from and pimped by James A. Joyce (see undersigned), a Star Chamber of cigar-chomping publishers charged with shilling a counterfeit *Odyssey*, numerous photobombs by characters copyrighted by Homer, and a Homeric heart attack. While the undersigned respectfully regret the author's coronary triple bypass surgery (performed by Timothy Hunter M.D., undersigned), it should not be conflated with the medical records of any mythological figure or author thereof, especially under the current catastrophic healthcare laws in the United States where preexisting conditions may not be covered. Further, Melesigenes, in his capacity as Homer, has raised a raft of objections to *To Banquet with the Ethiopians*, asking, for example, how something called "A Memoir" could bear so little relation to biographical fact. The author's father, Melesigenes points out, while Homeric, is not Greek; and his mother, while a goddess, is not, regrettably, immortal. Due to a conflict of interest with signatories such as the author's family, publisher, and other parties, Melesigenes has graciously declined to append his suit as a rider to this document. However, he reserves the right to pursue a separate action.

3. The Muse is of course extant, fully individuated, and eternally indubitable. Inexplicably, she is not undersigned. Presented with this petition, her bejeweled hand froze. Urged to deny any social, psychological, or physical congress with the author, her ambrosial lips trembled. Such reticence, we admit, is uncharacteristic, since she brazenly confesses to a shocking number of hookups with fellow signatories and a host of others. Frankly she can't shut up about it. But perusing *Phantom Signs*, the trollop became distraught, requiring physical restraint and heavy sedation. Several diagnoses have been put forward. After hacking the author's hard drive and finding some disturbing early drafts of the manuscript's subtitle, including *Death of the Muse*, *The Muse Dies in Universe City*, and *The Muse Is F(UC)ked*, our IT committee has released a memo to the effect that Universe City, with its canons, codes, bureaucracies, and proscriptions, is the source of the Muse's distress. Abstracts have been submitted suggesting that the author's contention that the Muse is archaic and should be re-

placed by "X" has flummoxed her. Around the nectar-cooler, gossips whisper about "Roba," where the author extrapolates, from an errant typo, a miraculous visitation. While Roba is, as claimed, a waterway in Ethiopia, it is also slang for a molly-bolt and a constellation in the pinwheel galaxy. The Muse needs to know this; but she does not wake, even when shaken.

4. The author's theme that poetry is a "Phantom Sign," poised between chirography and utterance with no native means of apprehension, that it therefore invokes absence, enters cosmic scale, and calls into being what he calls "nought," is contradicted by the very publication of this text and our captive presence herein.

5. Speech song is a crude redaction of H. L. Hix's complex argument; nor is Hix, as represented here, a cowboy. Hix's plight, along with that of William Heyen, J. Michael Lennon, Carol Moldaw, Robert Mooney, Steve Oristaglio, and D. M. Spitzer (all undersigned), is especially sympathetic, as they are published by or closely associated with the author's literary press, and therefore in no position to contest howlers such as the proposition that Moldaw's novel is actually a prose poem, or that Heyen conspires in a cabin in upstate New York to collapse the universe from three to two dimensions, or that Spitzer isn't the author of his own book.

6. At no time drunk or sober did the author's father, undersigned, mistake Queens for Galway, nor did Galway Kinnell, also undersigned and especially irate, transmogrify during a graduate seminar into a bear, malgré his iconic poem by that name. He is, however, in full possession of the semicolon and ready to use it.

7. Joyce and Shelley never waitressed in an Irish bar. The author's wife, while possessing selkie-like tendencies, is not now, nor has ever been, trans-species; nor is the Greek Professor (unsigned to avoid scandal) a sea nymph. All this is bollox.

While we do not doubt that at the time of this writing the author lives, he must resign in the foreseeable future from the subcommittee of breathers, while *Phantom Signs* may persist, even if remaindered, long past his transition. It's not that we object to writing per se, or to the perpetuation of our fame and memory in written form. But to be deprived of the dulcet cadences of the Muse, who lies in demented sleep; to be squeezed into sentences which yearn to dissolve into breath; to be marginalized between sign and utterance; to be robbed of a sublunary dimension: this we find unacceptable and we protest in the strongest terms.

In Solidarity,
Chinua Achebe, Achilles Son of Peleus, Aeneus Founder of Rome, Aeolus God of Winds, Theodor Adorno, King Agamemnon, Telemonian Ajax, Alexander the Great, Dr. James Andrews, Nin Andrews, Anonymous Outside Reader for UT Press, Aristotle, Matthew Arnold, Sheriff Joe Arpaio, Margaret Atwood, W. H. Auden, Joan Baez, Kelly Bancroft, Mikhail Bakhtin, Amiri Baraka, Matsuo Bashō, Charles Baudelaire, Nancy Woodridge "Sylvia" Beach, Old Woman of

Beare, Bellerophon Son of Glaucus, Jorge Mario Bergoglio (Pope Francis), John Berryman, Black Ice, William Blake, Madame Helena Petrovna Blavatsky, Leopold Bloom, Molly Bloom, Robert Bly, Giovanni Boccaccio, Officer Joe Bolton, Daniel Boone, Dr. Zack Bowen, Ray Bradbury, Anne M. Brady, Phelim Brady (Bard of Armagh), Philip W. Brady, Capt. Samuel Brady, Robert Browning, Kobe Bryant, Charles Bukowski, Richard F. Burton, Davy Byrnes, George Gordon Lord Byron, Stephen Cade Esq., Gaius Julius Caesar, Calypso the Nereid, John Casey (Sean O'Casey), John Charles Carter (Charlton Heston), Sir Roger Casement, Cassandra of Troy, Gaius Valerius Catullus, Willa Cather, ENS Charon, Noam Chomsky, Yi-Fen Chou (Mike Hudson), Jesus H. Christ, Cinderella, Circe Daughter of Helios, Liam Clancy, Paddy Clancy, Tom Clancy, Lucille Clifton, Hillary R. Clinton, James Connolly, Joseph Conrad, Gabriel Conroy, Gretta Conroy, Hart Crane, Cuchulain of Muirthemne, Philip Dacey, Roger Daltrey, the Dalai Lama, Dante Alighieri, Maurice Darantiere, Kim Davis, Thomas Davis, Stephen Dedalus, The Delphic Oracle, Demodocus of Phaeacia, Emily Dickinson, Dionysus God of Wine, St. Dismas, Rachel Dolezal, John Donne, Denis Donoghue, Hilda "H.D." Doolittle, Man of Double Deed, Rita Dove, Doug Ducey, E. I. DuPont, Robert Duncan, Iosif Vissarionovich Dzhugashvili (Stalin), Humphrey Chimpden Earwicker, Sr. Miriam Eileen, Dr. Albert Einstein, George Eliot, T. S. Eliot, Richard Ellman, AB Elpenor, M. C. Escher, Robert Fagles, John C. Farrar, Fearless, Samuel Ferguson, Timothy Findley, Tim Finnegan, Steve Francis, Robert Frost, Michael Furey, Rory Gallagher, Tess Gallagher, John Gardner, Georgia Me, Gestas (the Bad Thief), Nikki Giovanni, Robert Giroux, Glaucus (Grandson of Bellerophon), God the Father, Oliver St. John Gogarty, Maud Gonne, Jorie Graham, Robert Graves, Draymond Green, Woodrow Wilson "Woody" Guthrie, Dafydd ap Gwilym, Hamlet Prince of Denmark, Hector Prince of Troy, Ernest Hemingway, Heinrich Heine, Drew Heinz, Stephen Hero, Hannelore Heyen, William Heyen, Elsa C. Higby, H. L. Hix, Tony Hoagland, Dr. Robert Hogan, Joseph Holloway, Istvan Homner, Joseph Hone, Timothy Hunter M.D., Icarus Son of Daedalus, Kyrie "Uncle Drew" Irving, Henry James, LeBron James, Marlon James, Alwin Lopez "Al" Jarreau, Erica Jong, Michael Jordan, James A. Joyce, Kim Kardashian, Nikos Kazantzakis, John Keats, Robert Keeshan (Captain Kangaroo), Hugh Kenner, Genghis Khan, James J. Kilroy (was here), Coretta Scott King, Rodney King, Stephen King, Galway Kinnell, Thomas Kinsella, Carolyn Kizer, Bill Knott, Professor Bernard Knox, Ted Kraker, Milan Kundera, Laocoön Priest of Troy, Archibald Leach (Cary Grant), Lemon, Dr. J. Michael Lennon, David Livingston, Lloyd the Ghost Barman from *The Shining*, John Logan, Chris Logue, Albert Lord, Robert Lowell, Mina Loy, Fray Luis de León, St. Luke, Martin Luther, Major John MacBride, Finn mac Cumhal,

Thomas MacDonagh, Cathal Buí Mac Giolla Ghunna, James Macpherson, Fergus mac Róich, Mr. Magoo, Norman Mailer, Tommy Makem, James Clarence Mangan, Mickey Mantle, Roberto Manzano, William Matthews, Countess Constance Georgine Markievicz, Karl Marx, Zachary Mason, Rory Masterson, Sean Masterson, Colum McCann, Paul McCartney, Emmanuel D. McCluskey, George "Spanky" McFarland, A. J. McKinnon, Daniel McMullen, Billy Meehan, Melesigenes (Homer), Brian Merriman, Pegeen Mike, John Milton, Mortimer Mint, Mobutu Sese Seko Kuku Ngbendu Wa Za Banga, Carol Moldaw, Molly the Cat, John Montague, William Least Heat-Moon, I. M. Mooney, Maureen "the Lass" Mooney, R. W. Mooney, Michael Moorcock, Larry Moore, Marianne Moore, McKinley Morganfield (Muddy Waters), William Morris, Van Morrison, Mos Def, Malachi Mulligan, Kuno Meyer, "Prince" Rogers Nelson, Kirk Nesset, Friedrich Nietzsche, Paddy Noonan, Edo Nyland, Joyce Carol Oates, Barack Hussein Obama, Conor Cruise O'Brien, Red Hugh O'Donnell, Michael Francis O'Donovan (Frank O'Connor), Odysseus King of Ithaca, Oedipus the King, Shaquille O'Neal, Stephen M. Oristaglio, Dr. Robert Bayley Osgood, Osiris King of the Dead, Ossian Son of Finn, Alice Oswald, Ozymandias King of Kings, Paris of Troy, Charles Stewart Parnell, Professor Milman Parry, St. Patrick, Paul of "Paul's Case," Padraic Pearse, Sir Robert Peel, Pelé, Samuel Pepys, Robert Pinsky, William Bradley "Brad" Pitt, Plato, "Cyclops" Polyphemus, Ezra Pound, Dutch Potter, Jom Potter, Laurie Powers-Going, King Priam of Troy, Mia Priebe, Nathan Pritts, Prometheus Son of Iapetus, Marcel Proust, Henry Pussycat, Thomas Pynchon, Speed Racer, Paisley Rekdal, Nancy Reagan, Ronald Reagan, Debbie Reese, Steven Reese, Rainer Maria Rilke, Rocket Man, Theodore Roethke, Princess Rosamond, Jerome Rothenberg, W. H. D. Rouse, Bill Russell, George "A. E." Russell, Ryan the Pomeranian Pup, Michael Ryan, J. D. Salinger, Robert D. San Souci, Sappho, Satan of Hell, Dr. Carl B. Schlatter, Erwin Schrödinger, Edwina Seaver, Francesco V. Serpico, Theodor Geisel (Dr. Seuss), el-Hajj Malik el-Shabazz (Malcolm X), William Shakespeare, Percival Bysshe Shelley, Richard Brinsley Sheridan, Adam Silver, Charles Simic, John Smelcer, Rose Carmine Smith, W. D. Snodgrass, Socrates, John H. Speke, The Sphinx, D. M. Spitzer, William Stafford, Sylvester Stallone, Henry Morton Stanley, Gertrude Stein, Scott Strasburg, Roger W. Strauss, Sir Philip Sydney, John Millington Synge, James Taylor, Opie Taylor, Johnny Temple, Alfred Lord Tennyson, Telemachus of Ithaca, Publius Terentius, St. Theresa of Avila, Thersites, Dylan Thomas, Klay Thompson, Henry David Thoreau, Thoth, Leo Tolstoy, Wolfe Tone, Xipe "Flayed God" Totec, Richard Tottel, Donald J. Trump, King Tutankhamun, Archbishop Desmond Tutu, John Updike, Luis Valdez, Liberty Valance, François Villon, Publius Virgilius Maro, Rebecca Walsh, Bruce Wayne (Batman), Mary Jane "Mae" West, Walt Whitman,

Oscar Wilde, Iman Jacob Wilkens, William Carlos Williams, Oprah Winfrey, Thomas Woll, Sir Thomas John Woodward (Tom Jones), Adeline Virginia Woolf, William Wordsworth, James A. Wright, Thomas Wyatt, Yahweh, William Butler Yeats, Joseph Yule (Mickey Rooney), Zarathustra, Robert Allen Zimmerman (Bob Dylan), Louis Zukovsky.

PHANTOM SIGNS

PART
1

FACE

THE BOOK I ALMOST WROTE

I almost wrote a book. I wrote almost all of a book. Nearly every word. I reached the end. I edited and revised. I wrote the book many ways. I wrote it many times. I wrote it in prose and verse. I studied it. I learned almost all of it by heart. I didn't write the blurbs or flap copy; you're not supposed to write them, or if you do, you pretend to be someone else. I didn't decide the ISBN or PCIP or list price. I did not design the cover or delineate the gutters or select the font. I did not choose my name. But of the words conventionally ascribed to the author, I wrote almost every one.

It was a book about a paradox.
    A. Writing a book is hard.
    B. It's supposed to look easy.
    As Yeats says, "A line will take us hours maybe / But if it does not seem a moment's thought / Our stitching and unstitching have been nought."
    My book took a long time. It began as another book altogether. "To Banquet with the Worthy Ethiopians: A Memoir of Life Before the Alphabet" was the working title.
    A memoir is especially hard unless you are famous, in which case you get someone else to write it for you, or at least edit. The other problem is that people hate being flattened from three dimensions to two, so there can be issues when you write about living people. They can write back.
    Not being famous, I had to write alone. And the people I made two-dimensional were dead or their faces were masked. The memoir was set in a Long Island Police Athletic League boys' camp. In the summer of seventh grade—which the memoir calls the summer of Item 265—I spent my first nights away from home. The summer was bad. Horrible. Not just the gruel and bugs and sweaty shorts and sandy bunks and endless games of war ball. Adolescent boys are cruel to anyone different, and I was different. As the book says,

My body grilled in Rouse-like sentences,
Elongating while resisting girth
Until the chest caved in and the fingers of one hand
Could encircle a thigh. The ears unhinged.
The cartilaginous right speared like an antler.
The left lobe drooped below the jaw.
Eyelids pinked. Lashes crusted.
The trunk roiled, mapping new pustules.
Bloody pus clotted morning sheets.

These aren't the words I wrote in the memoir. I've lost those words completely. This is a later verse interpolation. But in every version the boys were hideous, and at the time it seemed that this was the only world I would ever inhabit: a nightmare landscape of terror and humiliation. The hoodlums promised that on the last night of camp they would all piss into a bucket and sneak into my bunk and pour the bucket over me. I ran to the camp office and made a collect call to my parents and begged them to come get me. They came. None of this is in any of the versions of the book I almost wrote, because I wanted to avoid dealing directly with those who were still extant. Instead, I focused on the Trojan War, and W. H. D. Rouse's prose translation of the *Iliad*. Thus the Rouse-like sentences.

For this paradoxical state of affairs (A & B) I blame Homer. Before he started to "articulate sweet sounds together" on the page, bards rocked and chanted, feeding the voice, and the voice fed the utterance. Or that's the way I had it in my book. But I wrote the book crouched over a screen with my eyes watering and sudden beeps from Facebook and my right foot going numb, and everything had to be constructed and verified and revised down to the nub.

Besides Homer, there were two other obstacles.

A. I had become a publisher. On the kind of whim that made Mickey Rooney launch movie musicals, I had started, with two cronies, a literary press. Etruscan, we called it, a little dizzy with self-delight. We schemed to use money from Stags, my rich friend, to hire labor while Mooney, my novelist friend, and I would select the books and meet writers and lunch at the Algonquin.

Then 9/11 happened. Bill Heyen, eminent poet and towering anthologist, proposed a book called "September 11, 2001: American Writers Respond." He wanted to capture America's first reaction to the tragedy. But Etruscan didn't, so to speak, exist. We had no distributor or designer or marketers or deal-cutters or editors. We knew about publishing the way foodies know about restaurants: we knew what we liked. But we did have Stags's money. So we hired a bright-looking lad and rented an office in Chestertown, MD. I was on sabbatical in Providence and had fallen head over heels for a woman 20 years younger and I saw everything as if through a sparkling veil and 9/11 didn't seem real. So we told Bill OK and he buttonholed 127 writers including John Updike and Erica Jong and Lucille Clifton and Robert Pinsky and he even made up a few writers like Edwina Seaver and Rose Carmine Smith with a wink to Joyce Carol Oates.

Then we contacted a pro named Tom Woll who had made his bones at Vanguard with Dr. Seuss back in the days of three martini lunches, and I met Tom halfway between Yonkers and Providence at a bagel shop on Rte 17 and Tom hooked us up with Mortimer Mint, a Dickensian refugee who made his fortune distributing the *Guinness Book of World Records*, and Morty sold ten thousand copies and we thought publishing was a cinch and then 8,500 copies came back— we didn't know about returns—and Stags coughed up more money and bailed us out.

By now I was a full-time publisher and people sent me manuscripts by the hundreds and we had to fire the bright-looking kid for fraud and I drove to the foot of the Chesapeake Bay Bridge and rendezvoused with our new managing editor at Hemingway's and handed over two armloads of files. Suddenly I was immersed in something I had always avoided: business. Now I could confab with my college pals about cost benefit and cash flow, and I learned that you can't treat employees like students because if students fail, so what? And manuscripts kept coming and I lost a few friends and some sleep and many of the poems were good, but not that good, or all good in the same way: a setting and observation about the setting developing into three or four related observations strung together in a short time span; usually walking was involved, sometimes driving. All were rectangular and they began to look like clumsy interpolations translated from Etruscan and it was mile after loose-stepped mile of chopped prose. Did I say all? Not so. Some were served straight from academic Delphi, where the oracle was deconstructed into semiotic salads only a tower-dweller could digest.

Poems are so enigmatic. Each emerges from some private darkness which publication does not entirely dispel. They are composed of such a paucity of words. We choose to trust their silences. But we approach with caution. No one wants to be taken in by a false poem. An accidental verse. So we screen them the way we screen blind dates. We hear from teachers or colleagues, reviewers and enthusiasts. We peruse the book: the colophon, the pedigree, the blurbs that confirm value with words like "luminous" and "sublime," the mysterious or catchy titles: *Return to a Room Lit By a Glass of Milk, Preface to a Twenty-Volume Suicide Note, Autonecrophilia, The Book of Orgasms,* or *What Narcissism Means to Me.* By the time we open the book and scan the creamy page with its noble Garamond, we are prepared to give each poem what William Stafford called "a certain kind of attention."

These conditions do not prevail in the publisher's office. Publishers receive only a brief cover and we must address the draft of the internationally unknown poet without the benefit of context. No private darkness, no magic, and certainly no rarity. There are thousands. They have no reticence. They come, as Philip Dacey says, "so encumbered."

Reading unsolicited manuscripts mars publishers. Print is limitless. If you are not a publisher, you may have no idea of how many serviceable poems are making their doleful rounds. At conferences or bars or beaches or subway platforms, we publishers pass one another and nod in silence, recognizing the vampiric gaze and slow shamble of the endless scroll.

Whatever their quality and number, these submissions were complete, and so they were better than what I was doing at my other desk, trying to write a memoir. Albert Lord who studied bards in Yugoslavia said that when oral poets learned to write, they lost the ability to compose spontaneously, and I thought that maybe something analogous had occurred and that after becoming a publisher I'd never be able to compose poetry again. And so I scribbled sentence after sentence until I was walled in, and the memoir was on the other side of the wall.

B. I have a love-hate relationship with sentences. I love the freedom and the buoyancy and the way they go on and on, executing a flip turn at the margin. But, they do go on. I compose them only in daylight or lamplight, always alone. They can't be learned by heart; they can't breathe for long away from print. They are—or at least my sentences seem—foreign. Sentences have no darkness. They are devoid of mystery. If you think of something that might go in a sentence, you stick it in. Bent on transposing whole cartons of toxic reality onto the page, you get woozy. Like I say, it's a paradox. So one day I went swimming.

I have a love-hate relationship with swimming. I love the freedom and buoyancy, the reach and kick. I love the glimpse of light when I suck in air, and the black lane lines refracting on exhale. I love the flip turn, and the full-stretch glide two beats long. At the finale, I speed crawl to the deep end and jackknife down to trace the tile insignia, staying as long as my lungs last, letting the rising take me, effortless. But a swimming pool is the place where I feel most alone, trapped in my mind. There's no end, no arc. Swimming doesn't correspond to anything I do anywhere else. Water is, finally, a foreign element which I cannot inhabit.

That October afternoon in 2010 I slipped into the chlorine water and began my regimen. But I got through only four laps when I felt pressure in my chest, and my breath went shallow. Later that day I was wheeled into St. Elizabeth's for coronary triple bypass surgery.

After a week in the hospital, I spent three months in my rocking chair by the fire, in the living room of our ramshackle cottage looking south on a park in Youngstown, Ohio, where I've lived for thirty years. Three decades, three months, three hours of unconsciousness. What matter? Youngstown is not home. That dreamscape has another name. I call it Queens. It's no Ithaca, my Queens—in fact it now doppelgangs Seoul and Baghdad, as once, in Father's voice, it was called Galway. Any destination, given time and distance, eludes naming.

At home in my rocking chair in the fall of 2010, I clutched the teddy bear with the cracked heart bib the nurses give heart patients to keep us from tearing the incision. I read, I binged on Netflix, I napped. Many patients, a pamphlet told me, feel depression when they return from heart surgery. But I felt peace. It helped that my wife was home and friends drove hundreds of miles to visit; it helped that I had colleagues to take over my courses and a managing editor to handle business at Etruscan; it helped that the autumn passed almost imperceptibly through the bay window facing the park. Life is good, I thought. And still think.

Then I turned to the pages that had been the memoir. How distant—a world glimpsed through fogged goggles. What matter what actually happened one summer fifty years ago? What matter, this breaking and remaking—wading through sentences that could never be heard at night or out on a walk; sentences that always needed light, and were always read alone?

And then, rubbing my bear's fur in my rocking chair in the autumn of 2010 deep in midlife, I began to rock. Back and forth, just as I had long ago in Queens in front of the hi-fi, rocking on hands and knees while Father's Clancy Brothers albums scratched unearthly tunes about a home so far off it might have been Ethiopia. Backward to the sea I rocked, forward into a world of goddesses and fiends.

As I rocked and chanted in Youngstown after surgery and dove deep to the bottom of memory-tracing runes, I began to see that there was no home, no element anyone could own or even belong to, except for a moment reaching for a single line. The reach is home, or hospital bed, and the line is the insignia of yearning. Scanning sentences, I knew that I didn't want to write a memoir to remake a vanished world. I didn't want my breath to go shallow. I didn't want to feel the way I had felt all those years ago with Rouse: knowing something lay beneath, some rhythmic present tense that sentences could only describe or obscure.

So I began my own translation: from sentences to lines. I started transposing history, as Timothy Findley says, "into another key, which is mythology." Backward toward Queens, forward into the Police Camp, I began to translate my sentences into blank verse—remaking or breaking or making up a life from a great distance—the distance of having been, briefly, dead.

From a page-bound home I rocked to a place where

> A child composes the rooftree of a house.
> Verse tunes his breath—iamb
> Of upturned face, caesura of sinews,
> The ache of denouement pricked by a 'huh'
> That triggers the next line. And within,
> Angle of toe and knuckle, cant of head,
> Each phrase devising its own signature.
>
> In the belly of a house the child soars
> Over the mountains and the wine-dark sea.
> Every plunge backward meets the thud
> Of flesh on bone, spurring the thrust forward.
> Heels anchor and the child has learned
> To quell time's surge with oceanic dream.

Writing is hard. It's supposed to look easy. But there's a third leg to the paradox: writing isn't even supposed to look like writing. It's supposed to seem like utterance. It's supposed to be heard, or overheard. It's supposed to appear as if it's from somewhere else. This is where the book I almost wrote was headed. It was about life before the alphabet, not just childhood, but the eons of myth-time before Homer started to write things down. A time when "eternity brightened the rim of each instant." Without the alphabet to keep time straight, everything could slide from now to forever and back in a generation or an instant. There was no breach between everything that happened and all that did not. Of course, it's another paradox to write a book about the futility of writing a book, though in many ways all books are about that. Sometimes I think that the last three thousand years of poetry compose a long elegiac wail for a time when "lines were conceived and spoken in one breath." And anyway, I didn't write a book about it. I wrote most of a book.

Years went by, and Etruscan grew and flourished and people kept sending me manuscripts and a few of them I published. Every month I finished a verse chapter. At the beginning of each month I almost drowned, overwhelmed by all I hadn't written, and by the end of each month I flew through the house. Over and over it happened, the drowning and flying, the rocking and chanting, till finally I was done. And because I had spent a decade reading manuscripts, I knew that this was different. It wasn't sentences. It wasn't chopped prose. I even changed the name. I called it, "To Banquet with the Ethiopians: A Memoir of Life Before the Alphabet." Nearly the same, but different.

I found Broadstone Books and Larry Moore introduced me to Buffalo Trace and the Kentucky Derby and he brought in a genius designer, Laurie Powers, to dress the words beautifully and we all edited and extrapolated and amplified and nitpicked and scoured the net for images and fonts. And one day a UPS box arrived at my house across from the park in Ohio. I tore open the carton and scattered the peanuts and inhaled the new book smell and caressed the gloss. My book. The book I wrote. I thought I'd written all of it. The whole thing. But I hadn't.

That night I read the words that had taken all those years and had finally broken through the wall of sentences. I read almost to the end, and it was strange because in this beautiful codex the words seemed as if they came from somewhere else and I didn't remember writing any of them.

Until I came to the second-to-last page. That's when I found out I had not written all the book. I wrote most of it. Almost all. But on the last second-to-last page, in the last stanza, I read a line I definitely knew I had not composed. A line I had never seen.

It was "Fearless fleeing naked toward Roba."

I knew Fearless. I knew he fled. But Fearless was running out of time into the sea. He was fleeing his body; he was swimming, he was almost drowning. Where was this unknown place, Roba?

It's a paradox to write a book about the way the alphabet walls us into our separate lives; it's strange to work so hard to make simple utterance.

In the beginning of the book the scrivener admits that his Homeric stand-in, Thersites, might just be an inkblot. Writing is hard. It's not trustworthy. It has the taste of death. And now it ended in a place I did not know.

I called Laurie and she sent me back a scanned page of the galleys which I had scrawled over and drawn arrows in. And in the margin, among the glyphs and arabesques, there it was.

"Fearless fleeing naked toward Roba."

Reading it now, as a late interpolator, I think the scrivener meant to say not Roba but "the sea" and he didn't mean the line to be there anyway, but somewhere else. But there it was.

That night I walked through the house feeling lost and overwhelmed as at the beginning of each month and it was even worse since I was a publisher and had dealt with all classes of screw-ups and had invented protocols and procedures and here was my book from another publisher and it was lost in some place I'd never heard of.

Then Laurie sent me a Google map. A map to this place that was invented out of a misread hand. A map showing that Roba is not nowhere. It is a waterway in Ethiopia, where Fearless was always trying to flee to escape the world, and time, and the boys at summer camp whom the memoir never names.

And that meant that the voice that Homer had heard and then silenced when he learned the alphabet and became a publisher, was still whispering, here, in this imperfect text.

Yes. Homer knew those waters. He had tried to swim out of his skin to Roba, Ethiopia. But who knows Homer? In the goodly company of the dead, he sways on a far shore. Truth? History? He is immersed in his own rocking and chanting. He is christened No One. His home, one ancient scroll declares, is called Ithaca. And Telemachus is his father.

It could be Homer was composed only of utterance and he made up his own father. It could be he never had a body. And what if he did? I know now that the body, like the alphabet, is a foreign element, composed of countless microbial beings swimming forever in the dark until the sternum is cleaved and the fugitives are brought to ghastly light.

Between what is called me and what is not, a child still rocks, composing the rooftree of a house. He reaches for Roba, like another element. He sings—I sing—as if this element were home, if only for a heartbeat.

NOTHING ATTESTED,
EVERYTHING SUNG

Contrary to rumor, I am not H. L. Hix. I understand the mixup. We are close in age. We are both tall, bespectacled Caucasians. Both poets, though of varying stature. My company, Etruscan Press, has published eleven Hix titles, one third of his output. Few buy and fewer follow. But I am not Hix. First, I am not composing a canon in dialogue with the Bible. Second, I am unlikely to get lost in an Irish bar, as Hix once did, missing an assignation to drink whiskey and discuss the publication of one of his books. I am disastrously familiar with this habitat. Third, H. L. Hix is a genius. It's not his fault; it's not a deal breaker. We've addressed the issue, man-to-genius. We're past it.

I first became aware that in some circles I was being taken for H. L. Hix during a conference call with Consortium, Etruscan's sales distributor.

"We wonder," said Eliot, "all these books by Hix."

"Prolific," I replied, "But this book . . ."

"Yes, but we are wondering at the office, you know."

"You'll really like this one."

"We have a pool."

"A pool?"

"An office bet."

"On sales?"

"We wonder if you are not you."

"Then who?"

"We wonder if perhaps you aren't H. L. Hix."

"I wrote all those books?"

"You've never been seen together."

"He's in Wyoming."

"Or someone else of the same name."

"Why me?"

"It would explain why you keep publishing unsalable books."

Another reason for the confusion is my tendency to steal from Hix. Quips mostly. Sometimes whole lines. The occasional groundbreaking idea—like song-speech—a paradigm representing poetry as a matrix of impulses: one toward linear movement, the other towards song's transcendent stillness. Poetry eludes song because it is never wholly present; transcends speech because it is never wholly lucid. Recently, for an Etruscan contest inviting a one-page submission from any genre, "a page that sings," I swiped "Nothing attested, everything sung."

It was easy. One afternoon I scrawled the slogan on a shamrock napkin and slid it across the bar to my friend Norman.

"What bullshit," said Mailer.

"What do you mean?"

"Nothing attested. I've got three thousand footnotes here."

"So?"

"And I'm not Norman Mailer, Batman. I'm his biographer."

The purpose of drinking whiskey in agreeable company—at least the purpose to which I will attest—is to blend. Taken in proper dosage, in the right ambiance, with select companions, and adjusting for various tastes, tolerance, and wallets, whiskey aligns homeostasis, producing concord. One indicator that blending has taken place is the commencement of song. Voices rise; identities dissolve. Attestation on the other hand signifies a failure to mix, a hardening of boundaries, the baring of fangs.

Faced with an ink-stained napkin, neither Mailer's biographer nor Hix's publisher sang. In fact, Norman Mailer does not, in nine hundred pages of *A Double Life*, sing once, though he attests much. His attestations are so persistently tumescent that they could never be mistaken for anyone else's. He is Mailer. Norman is he. The moniker itself parses—both fore and surname suggesting armor. H. L. Hix, on the other hand, is titrated to the fewest possible characters, none round. On the cover of his current book, *I'm Here to Learn to Dream in Your Language,* his name sinks into earth tones. On his next book, it may vanish or explode. The book after that will be completely gaseous. In Wyoming, the personage designated by the name rises, per legend, and straps on Carhartt overalls to scrive in a barn studio. Then he mounts a treadmill and pounds six miles of *Paradise Regained* before cruising Wyoming 80 to a red schoolhouse, composing with his cigarette hand. Few—fewer even than his readers—know this verse avatar's given name.

Norman brandished a finger. "I had six graduate assistants. We logged every step from Ashtabula to Zaire. Ninety-seven hundred index cards. Eighteen hundred interviews. Lawyers, agents, editors, wedding planners. We sacked the Flatiron Building. Pulped a quadrant of rainforest."

Gardner piped in. "Much depends on the convergence of theme and incident." He brushed pipe ash from his elbow patch and downed a jag.

"Fiction expands within limits imposed by the moral universe. The cleft between the seen and the believed makes art, whether biography or novel. Forget that, and you become a didact like Hix, or a glorified pornographer—like you, Norman."

Mailer's finger jabbed Gardner's Bly–white halo. "Moral Fiction, my ass. Stick an "is" in there."

"I'm Gardner's protegé, by the way," protested Gardner. "Paul is dead."

"You mean John."

"That too."

The use of inverted commas goes back to Luther. "I cite," we attest; "Therefore he is." Citation encompasses reference, encomium, or accusation. I have selected all these words from the hoard first coined by others but I do not own them. Joyce feared quotation marks, perhaps because he couldn't see them. Hix eschews quotation altogether. If I attest that he exists (and who will vouch for me?) my evidence comes from no attestation. It's what made the Romans fall for the Etruscans, a tribe they conquered but couldn't comprehend. The words don't fit the world, they suit the measure.

Hix was the first Etruscan. His groundbreaker, *As Easy As Lying,* maps hardscrabble routes between postmodern and New Formalism. Few follow. Fewer buy. Like the Romans, Americans find the artifacts of the conquered obscure and edifying.

I am not Etruscan by birth but I have been known to borrow from the corpus of H. L. Hix. Organs mostly. On the occasion of the Irish bar, I was thinking of nipping his liver. The operation is less drastic than it sounds since the organs themselves exist only in medical charts. To excise, it is sufficient to bracket the target organ in quotation marks. Hix's "liver" is pristine, virtually Promethean. I would not, however, touch his "spleen," which is calamitous.

The Romans couldn't read Etruscan but thought the liver was the seat of genius. One side effect of drinking whiskey while hosting an exceptionally bright internal organ is spatial-temporal displacement. Afternoons commenced in Irish bars wend to the parish of Ozymandias. On this particular day, had I bummed the liver, I might have said, "Norm luv, I don't know if Hix sings. From his performance in Irish bars, I doubt it. Song in inverted commas doesn't mean 'barbaric yawp.' It doesn't mean 'crooned,' or 'ululated,' 'diddly-eye-died' or 'full-throated' or 'recitatived.' Song doesn't come from somewhere else. It emerges, sourceless. So your nine hundred pages . . ."

"947 with index and bibliography." Norman stirred in sleep.

"Your tome."

"They made me cut ninety thousand words."

"Your opus."

Norm snored.

"The beauty of your beast—Mailer's best book, the book he lived—wasn't in his armor, or his bibliography, or even in his sliver of history. It was your song. It was the grace notes between the footnotes. The thrum beneath the sentences. Even the title: a paradox, a door into the dark. Throughout the varied pages I hear it: carol of wind tickling his hirsute paunch; chord of Jew's harp plucked in his Village flat; creak of distending wings; whistle of Viking axe that cleaved his bypassed heart."

"Those weren't in my book."

"Nowhere else. Your book is the rooftree of the house composed of song. Your book is the bright container. *A Double Life* attests to song. Phrases riff; phonemes carry tunes; the sewn spine rocks and the glossy snapshots chant. In your book, Norman Mailer wakes to the prime syllable of *The Naked and the Dead*; he surveys the East River where loom *Armies of the Night*; on the morning before his soul infected the sperm that fattened into Gore Vidal's nemesis, he yearns silently toward the final page of your codex, which is blank."

"The signature page."

"Your signature. Is it a prologue? Riverrun, you know. Tomorrow morning when your eyelids unglue and you stumble into the bathroom and gulp aspirin, when your cough goes basso profundo and your prick rampant, I wonder if you won't wish yourself transposed into the pulp of chirography, of signs, of silent vocables. Would you not be your book? Does Norman Mailer exist anywhere else? Don't tell me about hosts of rambunctious microbes. That necrotic iteration dissolves slowly underground. Now there is only Norman in the bar; soon there will be only Norman's book. Finally, a body composed of microbial footnotes. The utterances—to the extent they remain unremaindered—they are Norman Mailer."

Regretfully, having confined myself to my own tissue, I did not so retort. Mailer did not wake.

At this juncture or another identical era Joyce sashayed to the table and bent forward, quelling breath. "Commendatore, your credit card . . ."

Over her bluish breast loomed a bespectacled poet.

"Harvey!"

The laureate hurled his Stetson on the sawdust floor.

"You've ripped me off for the last time, Liberty."

I plundered my groin pocket. "I swear I didn't take it."

"Nothing attested, huh. You think a graphomaniac won't miss a few words?"

"Oh, that."

"Shelley ran my AWP card and found the napkin."

"Just one loanword." I mimed the inverted commas tattooed on Joyce's bosom. "That's not Shelley."

Hix kicked Gardner's ankle. "What's this bogman doing here?"

"He's ornamental. Here to attest that he was here. When these sentences transmogrify into song he'll disappear."

"That's just like you, Uriah. Attesting in my Word docs. I've seen you tiptoe around the hieratic umlauts; sweat-staining the serifs. You hijacked Eighteen Maniacs. Stuck a toothpick in Fray Luis."

"Harvey darling." My eyes wheedled. "I'm on task. Editing, vending, budgeting, tweeting. Look, read my sales notes." I pulled out a swatch of index cards and dealt them on the bar.

"#1 The project of Hixian Studies is to complicate identity by blending voices. Or forms.

"#2 In *Shadows of Houses*, selected lines reappear in predetermined order based on the Mayan calendar. In *Chromatic*, a vatic voice speaks from near death

"#3 in a prose villanelle. *Incident Light* interrogates a strange revelation; *As Much As If Not More Than* (*AMAINMT*), is

"#4 culled from Hix's most ambitious project, in which he interviews every person in America who has published at least four lines of verse, except

"#5 me (thus fueling the rumors). The result, *Alter Nation*, is unavailable from Ugly Duckling Press, run by cool dudes from Brooklyn.

"#6 They're password protected (book and borough). Out of this ur-text, Hix constructed the mythos of *AMAINMT*."

Gardner listed south. The deck of cards collapsed.

"Where's the rest, Slim?" asked Hix, scanning the sawdust.

"That was my last card."

"What then?"

"It's a conference call. Two minutes per title."

"Why don't you plan ahead?"

"This way they think I have more."

"Christ on a stick."

"That's another market."

Between inverted commas and impenetrable Etruscan is boustrophedon, a script without the interruption of spaces or vowels or prejudice toward left-brain reading habits. Boustrophedon is a helix, like Times Square, but unlit.

In Hix's next book, *American Anger*, the testimony collected from three centuries of class, gender, and race oppression is paved beneath the primary verse in boustrophedon, a ribbon endless as Wyoming 80. The book after that is *Rain Inscription*. It is writ entirely in water.

"Listen, Magoo," Hix said. "I'm only here in this dump you call your brain because I have another new book."

"Then it must be Tuesday." I studied Hix's silver belt buckle. "Can you write without a liver?"

"Here's the pitch. I have no name." Hix flicked Norman's ear. "Dumbo has nothing but. And why is he sleeping in a bar?"

"I've found it optimal to sedate my fictional characters when they are not performing necessary functions."

"So my next book will be the Collected Works of Norman Mailer."

"That's a lot of pulp."

"Print is ecologically incorrect."

"Whew. That saves $4.18 a unit, not to mention warehousing. Digital?"

"I won't support corporate hoods who steal names from South American rivers. My book will feature everything Mailer ever wrote reconstituted, distributed, and promoted in the breath of all Etruscans, including interns."

"Copyright?"

Hix sniffed. "Capitalist bollox." We'll "publish" Mailer's Collected without recourse to attestation. Also, mixed at random with Mailer's canon will be everything he never wrote."

"I smell crowdfunding."

"Brilliant!" said Harvey. "You must be H. L. Hix."

FACE

Kirk Nesset has no face. It's not just that his page is erased; he has lost face in every way imaginable. He has resigned tenure. His passport is suspended. His computer is monitored. He will probably lose his dog—a mini-Pomeranian he cradles in a sling. He may go to prison where his cred will not be high. Kirk Nesset's face dissolved the day the FBI raided his house, confiscating 500,000 files of child pornography. The children were named and categorized. Allegedly, Kirk Nesset confessed to preferring ages nine to twelve.

In twenty years, I've met Kirk Nesset three or four times. We've chatted in elevators and conference bars. He is handsome, charming, and flamboyant. The mini-Pomeranian is named Ryan, and he has his own Twitter feed. Or had. Ryan may lose face too. Kirk was fifty-seven years old when the agents knocked, but considering he had collected half a million files, it must have been some time since he started living a double life.

I am not leading a double life. Am I missing something? Am I living a half-life? Though of course if I were leading two lives, I wouldn't say so here. "I may not tell everyone. But I won't tell you."

Kirk Nesset was a writer. Weird to say, *was*, but he's facing a five-year mini-mum sentence and if he writes again it will be as another person. Oscar Wilde maybe. Or Michael Ryan. Writing, it has never been more clear to me, depends on a fictive persona with a real address. The writer must be someone. It's a myth that dead writers do better. As a publisher with four deceased writers on my list, I assure you that dying is a bad career move—unless your death makes a splash, and if you can splash, why not live? Revealing your double life might work, as long as your spare life qualifies for Oprah.

Kirk Nesset was leading a very creditable first life. He won the Drew Heinz Prize. He was a full professor at Allegheny College. His latest book is called *Saint X*, and, before his face disappeared, he had arranged a national tour. On the cover of *Saint X* is a picture of a child at midnight standing before a wading pool. Eerie and compelling—when Kirk Nesset was a writer. Now it's Exhibit B.

Kirk Nesset did not do the worst thing possible. It's worse than that. He *is* the worst thing. On the homo sapiens ladder, consuming child pornography is the lowest rung. It's beneath murder, which has a long pedigree and inspires awe. Each of us has witnessed thousands of staged murders. Murders make histories, careers, and literary genres. Murder is, at least in its initial phase, performed with others.

Theft? Cary Grant played a thief. François Villon was a thief. Christ's neighbors on Calvary were thieves. Thievery, like murder, has a profile. Both require action, entail risk, perhaps even demand skill. But this: performed in greenish dark, withholding of discourse, paralytic, masturbatory.

Wherever Consumption of Child Pornography sits in the cornices of evildoing, it is near the core of what the Jesuits called sin. In the words of that magnificent sinner John Logan, it is "an offense against love." Or against engagement. Against witness. Against, even, identity.

Kirk Nesset, of course, knew all this during the years he accumulated his collection. What was it like—closing the door behind him, abandoning all hope? What scruples did he need to relinquish?

I do not lead a double life, (the acolyte doth protest too much, methinks) but I have slid close to the edges of my single one. I have witnessed sin. Taken note. I have sinned. I sense your swelling interest, but I will not tell *you*.

I imagine that Kirk Nesset took note of all that we know about trespass. I imagine that he knew that the children whose images he downloaded were victims. I imagine this because when the FBI showed up, he confessed immediately and provided details about the nine- and twelve-year-olds. None of that "They think I'm mad" crap.

Kirk Nesset's Facebook page has been disappeared, but not before the discussion of his crime went viral. There are no "likes." Comments express shock and betrayal. Betrayal of the children, but more of Facebook friendships. How close to home he struck: "We had 238 friends in common." Several posts made it clear that whatever distinction might be drawn between making and consuming child pornography was spurious.

For some, Kirk Nesset's arrest triggered personal trauma. There were testimonies of rape, exploitation, and abuse. I was not surprised by these revelations. It is a fact of my own single life that nearly every woman with whom I have been intimate has suffered abuse, harassment, kidnapping, or rape. Am I crazy? Do I attract victims? Having only the one life, I don't know.

There are no rapists or child molesters on Facebook. In fact, there are no sinners—the most culpable are those who are squicked by the ice bucket challenge. But many are sinned against. Sometimes as individuals—but more often as members of a group. And this makes sense: isn't testifying to being sinned against a way to gain face? Sinners are secret, and if exposed, as Kirk Nesset has been exposed, lose both faces. But to be sinned against, in public, is to be saved.

When I told Kirk Nesset's story to a friend, he said that he didn't understand what glitch in the genome would turn someone's sex drive to children. It went without saying that he and I were driven by forces barely within our control that happen, in our cases, to operate within legal strictures. My friend's sigh was an acknowledgement that he was lucky to be so genetically encoded. But he, like me, has not been sinned against. At least not grievously. We might feel different had we been the children violated.

The children had a second life too. But it was imposed upon them. Now they must carry the second life, secretly, inside. Can testimony heal? Is that what we call shame—the light that exposes the second life? I can't decide.

Is the second life—if it is chosen willfully and in full possession of one's first life—the only place one can truly decide? Must all real choices be made in a chosen dark?

For instance, every day Kirk Nesset had a choice: he could act in a way he knew was wrong, or he could act rightly. Five hundred thousand times or so, he chose wrong. I don't know how often he chose rightly. Maybe never. Maybe only once. But even so, that choice now belongs to the Commonwealth of Pennsylvania.

Is all this too. . . . Jesuitical? What about the suffering of the children? Suffering endured in the dark, now brought to light. They had no choices. Choice—whether in dark or light—is a privilege. Privilege is elitist. I am ashamed.

But I have no choice. Here on the page, there is just one life. Every moment flattened to transcription diverts time's stream and radically distorts the scale of things. Inscribed, pain has no scale. Kirk Nesset's face takes up more of this sentence than the suffering of half a million children. If we insist on measuring suffering accurately, we must stop writing right now. Stop reading. Right now. No longer make the weaker argument the stronger. Unsuspend disbelief. No more bookwrights. Proscribe chirography. Let nothing mean or be but that which it is. Or if you must write, draft ordinances. Draw up manuals. Scratch out equations. Indite Chinese fortunes or French criticism. Do not write as if to conjure a body out of two dimensions, do not rip story from the ear, or song from the vibrant throat. Do not pretend to bring to life a human being. Because whatever suffering we reify in print, it is not the worst. It is never the worst. Writing drives everything crazy. Even the Jesuits. "If all evil," they wrote, "could be erased by the permission of one venial sin, still God could not permit."

If we insist on scale in suffering, we must heed Theodor Adorno's adage, "To write poetry after Auschwitz is barbaric."

If Kirk Nesset's impending incarceration seems to me barbaric, it is not only because he is, like me, a privileged white male in middle age, but also because I have just come from my writing class at Trumbull County Correctional Institute. Our next assignment is to compose in one stanza a cell, a task which I imagine the students will perform with profound intimacy. "The cell is gray," one student might begin. "The cell is three steps endless," says the incarcerated surrealist. "The cell is the pin of my skull's grenade," screams the escape artist. "The cell is an eternity of daybreak in the suburbs of Juárez, Mexico," writes my incarcerated James Wright. But the cell is not a book. I can't imagine it. If I imagine Kirk Nesset confined in this unimaginable space, I am imagining myself.

I have met Kirk Nesset three or four times; this I have confessed. But that was at the beginning of these sentences. Writing can commence in open air, but the pressure of line upon line snuffs out light. For you, ten minutes have passed. You are home in late afternoon in an endless October and the plaid recliner prickles the shoulder blades and a wing-shaped shadow plays on thumb and forefinger and into the crease of the spine of the book that is there and not wholly present, a thing you have picked up without intending and may put down this moment, as if bidden.

In my cell, the ashtray is full and the lightbulb has seared my retina and I have not slept. And while I continue to deny the second life of which I have, I swear, no knowledge, I will stipulate that my first meeting with Kirk Nesset was not casual. It took place at a job interview for a position as assistant professor at Allegheny College. Kirk Nesset chaired the search committee. I didn't get the job. The sinecure was one of a number of Kirk Nesset's privileges that I have been denied: good looks, a pinch of literary fame, a dog. Am I choleric? Do I now feel karmically redeemed? I can't decide.

With karma, you never know. Maybe Kirk Nesset will write a memoir. In memoirs, the protagonist may be a dope fiend, or murderer, or even a child pornographer—though no memoir that I know of has plumbed that depth—but the name on the glossy cover spells success. Pornographer or memoirist? Like Schrödinger's cat, it's neither until you open the box.

I am a publisher—I open the box. I facilitate the illusion that the writer is completely other, so immersed in the second life she cannot be reached except by someone else's hand turning the doorknob, some agent of One Life sleuthing half a million files. Only by my presence can you enter another's dark. I make the dark inviting, tantalizing, safe. If you don't believe me, read my flap copy.

But watching me opening the cell into the writer's dark is never enough, is it? You want to open it yourself. You want to violate the dark. You want to see the drafts, variorums, notebooks, letters, diaries. You want to be there. You want to insinuate yourself into the moment before nothing was written into existence. Before identity. Before anything could happen. I understand.

I stay because I know that failing to gain access, you'll buy. You'll shelve a title in your library, or place it, as if casually, on your coffee table. Its gloss and blurbs and colophon and Garamond draw the eye and gratify the touch. But deep down, something's missing. Something has been covered over. Something writers would not willingly reveal.

How do I know? I confess, I have a double life. I am not only a publisher. I am a writer. I do not publish what I write. The cells are separate and discrete.

In one cell, I tear open the carton, let peanuts fly. I press the book to my face, inhale the new product aroma. I feel the sturdy but fragile clothbound edition, admire its heft. I touch it all the way down, the spine's indentation not unlike the curves of a human spine. The creak of the first opening, the slight resistance, the feeling of the thirty-pound bond, acid free. I love the book. I love the books of others, and I love the books other publishers have made out of my writing. I port them in my cargo pants; I drool on them in bed.

Then, to underline, to annotate—how reckless. The first dog-ear. The beer ring. The warp after a day left on the ledge of the car's back seat. One day you pick up the book as if it came from someone else and realize that the cover is garish. The font is skimpy, the colophon obsolete, and the author pic has morphed to Opie.

In the cell of my second life there is no book. And no light to read by. Sometimes, I feel a presence at the keyhole. I shiver and squirm. Is someone there? Will you ever come? Do I want you to come? I can't decide. In this cell I know why Virgil and Joyce burnt their drafts and why Salinger fled and McPherson impersonated Ossian and Frey lied to Oprah. What were they doing, but squirming at the light and the prying eyes?

Are writers bad? Plato says so. Hell, with Socrates as a cellie, I'd take hemlock too. But are we bad all the way through—with a capital B, as in Bukowski, Baudelaire, Byron, Berryman, Boccaccio?

Are we the worst? True, we have the second life here—not on your page but on mine—blank, scratched on, accusatory. But we'll come forth if asked, usually. And for all the apocrypha about found manuscripts and forgeries and interpolations and salacious correspondence, I—the writer, not the publisher—monitor the transition into light. I choose the shape and depth of shadow. And you, reader, feel the shadow, though all you have seen is the chimera I have shaped.

What we want is not just fresh awareness but the illusion that we have been allowed into a darkness of which the writer himself is not truly aware, just as I allowed him to slip gender into the sentence, as if unseen. That's the real, unmediated him, you think.

I have turned Kirk Nesset back into a writer, no? I have compared his half a million crimes with innocent scribblings. Not in real life. In real life, Kirk Nesset is going to prison where he can enroll in one of my classes. But here on the page there is no scale. And everything is like everything else.

I have met Kirk Nesset three or four times and now you are wondering if I am breaking under the weight of all these sentences. Suffering has no scale? Let the world burn for one untended sin? I sense your frustration. You've pushed this far and no confession.

I confess that behind the face I see tunnels. Passing through eyes, light takes on shapes. It may not matter who or what they are. Their passage haunts, no matter what they've done, no matter what you've done, no matter who I think I am. I think the passing of these specters makes it possible for us to write at all. And makes it impossible and necessary. I think that, finally, Terence, not Adorno, was right. Nothing human is alien to me.

But what about something monstrous? And is this sentence human? If I am leading a double life, one half of it does not exist.

The friend to whom I told Kirk Nesset's story asked why I was writing about it. Do I think I am Kirk Nesset? Am I crazy? Won't readers assume that my attention and empathy, my canny failure to condemn, indicates that I too am a pervert? Do I really think writing is like child pornography? Do I care about my good name? Step off, he said. Walk away.

But I can't. And I know you are still waiting for a confession. You are patient. You monitor, you stake out, you wiretap. And I will break. I am breaking now. I deliver my confession. First I wrote it in French, then in boustrophedon, then in water and finally here on this page in a hieroglyph so vaporous that only those who have surrendered to their second life can see it.

So read:

If you have seen—did you think you were the only one? Did you think you were original? Are we absolved?

And if you have not seen, are you relieved? Ashamed? Are you pressing your eye to a dark keyhole? For you, I give this redaction of my confession in plain English:

Once, long ago, with a loved partner, I failed to bring to term a child. There is no adequate word in plain English, which is why you need a second life to understand. Without a second life, reading in plain English, you may think I equate child pornography with abortion; you may think I'm a pro-life nut. You may unfriend me. But there is no child.

Everything I have done is at the lip of that darkness. Nothing has scale. What happens here in the darkness has no consequence for the living. I do not think this confession satisfies you. I am not going to prison. Still, I have made the weaker argument. I have disappeared my child.

Three or four times have I encountered Kirk Nesset. How else to say it? First on the occasion of my job interview for a position of assistant professor at Allegheny College. This we have established. The interview took place at MLA in Chicago, and the walls of the interview room were greenish white. Most MLA interviews take place in hotel rooms—unsettling enough, with the towels crumpled and toilet gurgling and a junior committee member perched on the queen bed. But this was not a hotel room; it was a classroom, with plastic chairs arranged around me in a horseshoe, and outside was the Chicago El and I could hear the wind whistling down Morgan Street into the future. Everything moved slowly. My answers were dry and stiff. My gestures seemed slightly out of sync like a dubbed movie. This was before Kirk Nesset adopted Ryan, and before *Saint X*, and before I bumped into him in the elevator or bar, and before I read about him as a consumer of child pornography. This was before I embarked on the life I'm leading now, here on the page, far from Allegheny College or anywhere else. But it was not before I failed a life, to which I have confessed, twice, above.

Composing people out of symbols is no crime, is it? I do not equate writing and abortion and child pornography. Maybe there is no sin. I can't decide. The child and the children haunt me but I cannot name them. The sin is nameless. The sin is naming. It is in the wind, out of sync. It makes it impossible to cleave to one life and keeps us locked in our separate cells.

It is mine own.

It is the children's. It is Nesset's before he became himself.

Jesuits and writers disagree about everything except one thing. Jesuits call it sin. Writers call it the second life. Both call it "Original."

THE MAN OF DOUBLE DEED

Being childless, my childhood has receded into myth.

I must have had parents and schlepped to school and played games and wept and laughed and yawned through Sunday Mass. But what I remember best is rocking in front of the family hi-fi. All afternoon, back and forth, I rocked to Father's scratchy Clancy Brothers albums. Goddesses and tinkers and book-wrights and spirit eels and the hated *Sassenach* and the hosting of the *Sidhe*—all hissed and babbled through the needled grooves. No words, only utterance. On hands and knees, speed adjusted to song, I soared over the streets. My heels kept me from regressing beyond Queens, but I embodied an oceanic voyage, finding in rhythm a charm against time's surge.

Rocking in front of the cabinet hi-fi I first heard the man of double deed. He made no sense. He befuddled all the senses, and he still does. He doubles and twists and dervishes. His seed becomes snow becomes birds becomes ship becomes stick becomes knife.

When I ask him, "Why don't I remember any words but yours?" the man of double deed croons, "Like birds lose words inside of song."

I have never seen the man of double deed. But I have heard him many times in my own voice.

"Let me sing him once," I say. "And you'll have him by heart."

No one—not playground of third graders, nor clutch of drunks, nor pride of grad students, nor sailors nor hedge funders nor inmates nor rest-home dwellers—has ever heard him twice, or needed to. No one has failed, after one hearing, to forget everything but the man of double deed.

At first they doubt.

"How can we know him after just one time?"

Then silence ripples, and the listening approaches the intensity of the moment before a thunderstorm.

The man of double deed enters the air. He is here and beyond. He is heard. Sometimes my arms join in and fingers peck to sow the seed, and dance in the air as the seed turns to a garden full of snow, and my hands flit like birds upon a wall and drift up turning to a shipwreck in the sky and whip down like a stick upon my back and finally clench a fist to plunge a penknife into my heart. And I am dead and dead indeed.

But I can't write him down. I might break the spell. I might lose him forever, the way Homer lost utterance when he learned to write.

When the famous Homer scholar Milman Parry asked an unlettered bard if it was possible to remember a nightlong poem after just one hearing, the bard nodded.

"Word for word?"

"Word for word."

The next night the bard spoke the poem, and Parry recorded it and compared it to the night before and it was the same poem but with completely different words. Like birds he lost the words inside of song. But when the bard learned to write, he created an original outside himself and lost the ability to compose. No longer could lines be conceived and spoken in one breath. Time and myth were cleaved. The light was silenced.

What's a word if it isn't written down? Until the alphabet locks them down in time, words are breath. They generate themselves. They are like William Matthews's waves—not water but a force that water welcomes and displays. Because he is not written, the man of double deed welcomes and displays all utterance, including several species of the dead indeed.

No one hears the man of double deed the same way, but two things always happen.

First, "Like birds it was upon the wall" always changes to "It was like birds upon the wall."

I have come to believe that my birds—they of the syntactic inversion—are a late interpolation, crafted by the children of Homer to exploit the dynamics of the alphabet. Acrobats of syntax are Homer's children, sleight-of-handers who know that the line gains strength by avoiding opening with three weak syllables. Homer's progeny love drama. "Like birds," they say, and for an instant the reader tingles with conflict and possibility.

But those who hear the man of double deed just once are not listening to anyone. They are raptured in cadence and the transubstantiation from early snow to late birds. They feel a force that language welcomes and displays.

It was like birds upon the wall.

The second thing is the shipwreck in the sky. Here, all the voices—the one in the back row and the one drooling on the bar and the one too cool for school and the one who hasn't really heard—all chorus together.

'Twas like a shipwreck in the sky. Of the seven images, this is the most striking. When all chime in on the sky shipwreck, I know that although we rock in time with the surf, we still adore the phantasmagorical world. The birds of aural imagination and the ship of visual imagination are both engaged. The man of double deed lives in both species. There is sound inside the light.

In his noble introduction to Fagles's *Iliad*, Bernard Knox says that each of Homer's dactylic hexameter lines displays the arrangement of the whole poem. Each begins with conflict and possibility, and proceeds through a variety of sounds to fill the metrical requirements. But each line ends with the same strict pairing of dactyl and spondee. The poem is inside each line—from possibility to finality. By the end of the *Iliad*, the force of the story has been welcomed and displayed sixteen thousand times.

The man of double deed is not sixteen thousand lines, he is fourteen—or so I imagine, since I've never counted. But he has been recited so many times now in so many versions that perhaps he nears sixteen thousand lines. How many knives have pricked his heart? How many deaths has he suffered or, perhaps, forestalled?

Once, a surgeon stuck a penknife in my heart and I was dead, but not indeed. There was sound inside the light. I was wheeled in and instead of counting down I recited the man of double deed. He sang that I was dead indeed which meant I would not be dead, since rhythm is a charm against time's surge.

Had I passed completely into myth, I might have recited all of Homer after one hearing.

"How do you remember all those words?" Charon would have asked.

"Like birds lose words inside of song," I'd have sung, rocking back and forth in his sky shipwreck.

I wasn't dead indeed but I was intubated for an eon and could sing only imaginary songs. So, Tuesday evenings from June till March, birds gathered upon a wall and since the man of double deed was too short, we migrated all the way from Stately Plump Buck Mulligan to Yes I said Yes I will Yes.

None was dead indeed or transcendent or even adept, so we required an outward sign. We needed one printed copy of *Ulysses*, in all its editorially disputed leaves. But because we never saw the man of double deed and because Homer never saw the *Iliad* and because Joyce was so blind he could hardly see Sylvia Beach, we shared just the one codex. We sowed the book until it turned to snow. One bird read. Then another, while the flock listened.

We listened for the sound inside the light. We listened until we heard the force *Ulysses* welcomes and displays.

Every Tuesday night two things happened.

First, Dublin and Ithaca crashed like a shipwreck in the sky.

Second, we heard what wasn't written: possibility and conflict yielding to illuminated sound.

Yes I said Yes I will Yes. Yes I said Yes I will Yes.

We heard it when it wasn't said. We heard it when it was.

It was a thrum beneath each unlineated line.

The final dactyl of the *Iliad* is "tamer of horses." In the *Odyssey,* "form and voice." *Ulysses*'s final utterance is "yes." With each new version, matter is doubled more fully into sound.

One Tuesday night a form and voice came from beyond the sky-wrecked dactyls, and I stepped out into the blindfolded night and there she was on the doorstep, sitting on her haunches: Molly Bloom.

She regarded me. I regarded her.

She was outside human ken until she spoke—the same syllable as her first utterance as Calypso. "Mn," she said, and stepped, tail high, into her name.

The closest I come to seeing the man of double deed is when I regard Molly Bloom from a distance of ten paces. We regard each other, pharaohically.

"What transpires, Molly?" I inquire.

Sometimes her ears turn toward the query and sometimes they do not.

Is she further than my childhood? Farther than Homer? Is she farther than the place I go to hear the man of double deed?

For all her fecund lexicon, Molly Bloom's first utterance as Calypso is still the one I hear when I regard our Molly: "Mn."

It is the sound missing from the last word I heard on the operating table. Its absence was the reason I wasn't dead indeed.

The surgeon who penknifed Joyce's heart is Stately Plump Buck Mulligan.

"Ah the Greeks, Dedalus," he intones. "You must read the original."

Dedalus trembles. Even the sea, in the original, is fearsome: snot-green, scrotum-tightening. But Homer had no original. *Ulysses* has hundreds of originals. Just ask Darantiere, the printer.

If you forget the words, remember song, and the world unfolds whole in every line. This is the force welcomed and displayed in the months I came back to life.

Humans do not own speech, even when we inscribe it. The page does not define words. Beneath Joyce's sentences are measures. Though he wrote thirty thousand different words, each contained what was not written down: the sleep inside the waking, the sound inside the light, the *mn* inside the deed.

Yes I said Yes I will Yes.

My childhood is myth, but Molly Bloom continues to take form and voice. She has been Calypso. She has been Penelope. She has been a calico cat. Today she is a five-year-old girl. Her given name is Mia. I introduced her father to the man of double deed and he passed him on to his young daughter. She heard him once, knew him right away, and made him hers, word for word.

Here is Mia's Man of Double Deed

There is a man of double deed.
He's in his garden sowing seeds.

When the seeds began to grow
'Twas like a garden full of snow.

When the snow began to melt
It was like a ship without a bell.

When the ship began to sail,
It was like a bird without a tale.

When the bird began to fly,
It was like an eagle in the sky.

When the sky began to roar
'Twas like a lion at my door.

When my door began to crack
'Twas like a stick upon my back

When my back began to smart
'Twas like a penknife in my heart.

When my heart began to bleed,
It was death, death, death indeed.

Those who fear the man of double deed fear the original. Homer had no original, and Joyce knew no Greek, and Mia has no fear. She has heard the force which the poem welcomes and displays. Her bird has no tale. Her Molly is a lion. She has spun the sound inside the light. She is *mn*.

Mia has released me from the spell. Now I can regard the man of double deed, knowing that this is only one version, only now and mine, and no original.

Here he is, as he was when I rocked in front of the hi-fi.

There was a man of double deed
Who sowed his garden full of seed.

When the seed began to grow
'Twas like a garden full of snow.

When the snow began to fall
Like birds it was upon the wall.

When the birds began to fly
'Twas like a shipwreck in the sky.

When the sky began to crack
'Twas like a stick upon my back.

When my back began to smart
'Twas like a penknife in my heart.

And when my heart began to bleed
Then I was dead and dead indeed.

Now close your eyes and rock. Meet him yourself.

BASKETBALL AT 60

I've been happy these days, moment by moment, and the mind that once roiled with lust and rage is tranquil. The big questions have all been answered. How will I do? Whom will I love? What will I untimely suffer? What dread fire?

But that's not all. I feel a presence. Not too close, not imminent. An impending shadow, out there in the zone of tinnitus or climate change. Age. I am on the verge of withering into truth.

Yet, at noon on Mondays and Fridays, I spread my leaves, grab my gym bag and trot to the rec center. I am playing basketball again.

It's been so long since I suited up that I don't know what to do with my bifocals or wedding ring. The shorts are bloomers, the jersey is an ad banner, and the clown-big sneakers swoosh. The nets are distant as Joyce's God; the floor is hospital parquet. There's even a three-point line (three is two in a game to eleven by ones).

But I'm back. Nothing has changed. And everything.

I don't feel old. If I woke alone in a strange bed, I'd have no notion if I were thirty or sixty. Pull the blinds and my prana could lounge through any of ten thousand mornings, teaching or biking or *bavarding* or banging the bodhrán sans calendar. I've lost no bandwidth of memory, no inch of height. I was already bald. I have no children or corporate ladder to notch years. My job is stagnant, my town timeless as Brigadoon.

But change is coming. By fall or slide or decrepitude or aphasia, in some nearly foreseeable season it will come. Age. The vestibule of null. I expect it, as I once anticipated manhood. And like manhood, it will arrive all at once.

But for now, I am ageless. Everywhere but here.

Of course, I'm not really playing, if playing means being in the game. Most basketball activities are no longer available to me. I can't sprint, or box, or shoot. I have no hops. Good thing I'm a lefty, since I can barely lift my right arm above my shoulder. My eyes seem ok, and from wrist to fingertip I'm unimpaired. And in this pickup game I'm still tall. I can slouch my ass down to Bethlehem and post up.

Who are these lunchtime hoopsters? They are the Quick. Neither moribund nor slow. For the Quick, the future is a distant rim, the past a no-look turnover. What transpires here and now—on the court, on earth—is all that counts: How good? How long? Always? Anyone else? For the Quick I am not ageless. I am a portent.

I look the part. Bald helps, but I bring so much more: bypass scar, droop eye, liver spots, cabbage knees. I jog as if through swamp. I am my own slow-mo replay. My countenance bears witness to campaigns beneath rusted rims. I am six degrees from Dr. Naismith.

The Quick take heed. They proffer no trash. Both sides cheer my rare scores. An intern paramedic asks if I'm all right. Through whole sessions I am unjostled.

Today, after yawning through my abbreviated up-fake and arthritic hook, my defender patted my ass. "Fundamentals, Old School," he purred. "Sound."

To the Quick, I am a semiportable totem.

After lunch, I hobble back to my desk, gulp Powerade, and lour. Now, I am an editor. Poetry editors are not quick. We plod. We stall. We are in daily congress with the ageless. So what if quick verses flash by? Let them break unmetrically and enjamb on a dime. When stanzas drive head down, when they fade from three for two, when they won't pass, I tap my comic-strip fedora and chomp my wraith cigar.

"Fundamentally unsound," I growl.

I pat *their* ass and sit them on the bench. Then I roll out the x's and o's.

"OK Speedsters, huddle up."

> They stroll through gentian and coltsfoot to the pond's edge,
> while last light silts the water. Dusk
> and Monet believes again this is his masterwork; that's why
> he stays; to be inside the painting unscrews

"Stop there, Ace." I tap the blackboard.

"Gentian? Coltsfoot? You're from Queens. They're just botanical symbols to you. And the line breaks? Sure, I get it: torquing the syntax, that stutter step. Yes, 'Dusk' at the margin wants to swallow all six beats. But where do you go from there? You've pushed the caesura out of bounds but haven't laid down the dream cadence. You're riffing off no pattern."

My fingernail screeches across slate.

"Past 'Dusk' the silence is so grave I'm shouldered out; I never catch Monet. It's all one direction. Only one thing happens."

I rap my knuckle on the line endings.

"*Dusk. Why. Unscrews.* They're real and here and now. You think they enjamb, but for me they end stop. I can't go back. I'm on an island out of time."

I swipe the board clean. "Next."

There is a place in far north Canada . . .

To lurch, crooning in moonlight from the pub . . .

Broke in my mother's country
where there are no woods . . .

"What's with the fakes, Rocket Man? Not faking, you say? You coughed it up for real? I get it, son. And why not say what happened, as Lowell asked? But Lowell first ran years of suicide sprints. His 'what happened' was a playoff; yours is a scrimmage.

"So stop. If it was real and true, say it in sentences. When Ezra said that poetry needed to be at least as well written as prose, he wasn't talking about grammar. He meant—or I say he meant—that sentences will always be our first way of stepping through the waking world. One on one on one. Forward. Capable of being seen. But they move in one direction. Lines have to offer something else, compassing return.

"Poetry isn't a set of conventions any more than basketball is an industry. It's a way of doubling, of being in and out. You play, and your mind sings, daydreams, makes love, or enters a dark forest. It happens once in sentences. But lines glide back and forth, above and below the rim. They are the present absence."

But I can't tell these rookies anything, any more than I could tell anything to that gunner who first scribbled those words—that is, the kid that was me so long ago.

It's not their fault, I know. It's me. I've lost my touch. I can't play the Quick. They are bright and earnest and freshly pixelated. But they are completely present.

They press full court. They charge both ways at once.

And they can't play me. To them, I am already bronzed.

My lunchtime game is different. It doesn't take place all at once. All the lunchtimes of the past close in. Because my legs are slow and my mind quick, one sneaker runs in the shade of *once* and the other paces alongside in the glare of *now*.

This poor forked animal trundling between tenses? *Once* it battled Mazembé under a Katanga moon; *once* it signed "Rick Barry" for skinhead hoops fans on a Dublin tram; *once* it played—really played—with spirit, sweat, and nerve—on this very court at lunchtime eons back, when flesh and soul were 'twined.

Only by grappling with *now* does *once* achieve final form.

The Quick sense this: in my rooted footwork and palsied dribbling they glimpse the form in which we all drift, quick and slow, toward agelessness, encompassing three decades and three hundred.

These are the mates I can play with. From a far *once* they utter *now*—the ultimate three for two by ones. And whether *once* took place in Troy or Lubumbashi or at Monday's lunchtime when a quick kid windmilled the winning score, without the ageless nothing can touch *now*.

So afternoons at my publishing desk I play the ageless, who are still quick. In this game, everything still counts.

The semicolon in the last quatrain of "Easter, 1916" still counts.

> We know their dream; enough
> To know they dreamed and are dead.

Does Yeats mean it is enough to dream? That we should believe the dream because the heroes died for it? Is Yeats the last romantic?

Or has he taken his talents to Team Modernism? Do we know only their dream? Do we know the dream only well enough to know that they did dream, distantly as the awakened know?

A comma tips it one way; a period the other. The semicolon keeps us waiting still, paused in the infinite fraction between "enough" and "to know."

The editor Richard Tottel, on the verge of scratching T. Wyatt's jumpy, spondaic "It was no dream, I lay broad waking" for the smooth, iambic "For it was not a dream, I lay awake" on the galleys of "They Flee from Me" in his *Miscellany*, still counts.

If he does it, the tabloids howl.

"Sir T kept it real," the blogs proclaim. "Wyatt's a genius. Tottel's a bum."

But what if the waking needs to be taken slow, as Ted Roethke tweets, so the body can glide ten thousand days at once. Maybe Tottel fears an untimely fracture.

As I still fear.

And Homer—nicknamed for some hobo ballplayer. Does he count? Somewhere between the quick success of his first book and the first draft of his second, with the banquets and tributes and guest appearances, he's lost his game.

The *Iliad* opens in sync with his Olympian coach. "Begin dreaming here," he commands.

Start at the point where Agamemnon, son of Atreus
That king of men, quarreled with noble Achilles.

By the time he pens the sequel, he's lost touch.

So now, daughter of Zeus,
tell us his story, starting anywhere you wish.

"Please, Muse," he's begging her, "Start dreaming anyplace. I don't know where I am. Please keep me in. I'll play with everything I have left."

Far into overtime these contests are still in doubt.

And in my hip-sore gait, in my trash-muttering, in my spastic bound—just maybe—the Quick will sense that nothing happens at once, and that everything now continues to season, and that even the ageless yearn and fear to age.

And them, the ageless? At lunchtime Mondays and Fridays, if they lean forward from the cheap seats of the Garden's blue heaven, they might still hear me gasp, "Keep me in. Play me the fundamental sound. Let me, for this one hour, count."

PART
2

KITH & KIN

COMMENCEMENT

Proud, joyful, tender, valorous. These are the words that pass through the mind of Gabriel Conroy, the protagonist of James Joyce's story "The Dead," as Gabriel descends the staircase following his triumphant speech at his aunts' Christmas dinner. With his beautiful wife Gretta on his arm, he looks forward to the night at the Gresham Hotel, where his literary labors will be rewarded.

And so we may feel today: proud of our accomplishment, joyful in our abilities, valorous in our hopes, and tender toward our own literary labors. Like Gabriel, we hope that our work as writers—the planning, drafting, shaping, and revising—is rewarded by friends, by readers, by publishers, and by reviewers— by, might we dare to dream—the world.

But, as you may recall, when their carriage arrives at the hotel and Gabriel and Gretta enter the well-appointed Georgian room, and he signals the porter to snuff the candle, and he calls softly, "Gretta dear," his thoughts of love and conquest are suddenly dashed and he is confronted by a specter—Gretta's memory of a lover from her past, a boy named Michael Furey, who died long ago at the age of seventeen for love of her. Conjured by a ballad, "The Lass of Aughrim," sung at the fête, the ghost of Michael Furey now stands between Gabriel and his triumph. His hopes are thwarted, but a new story—one in which we ourselves are invited to partake—now opens.

Pride, joy, tenderness, valor—success is wonderful. But ultimately, it's predictable. All happy families, Tolstoy tells us, are alike, but every unhappy family is unhappy in its own way.

Great writing never ends in triumph. In fact, great writing doesn't begin until our original intention has been snuffed out and we are confronted with the specter of the other, as Gabriel is confronted with the dead.

This year we have witnessed in our presidential election the thwarting of expected success on a global scale. Whatever your political views, it's hard not to think about the personal consequences of failing so grandly in public. I think we know what Donald Trump is feeling—but what about Hillary? For writers, failure is just so much more interesting than success.

Yeats puts it this way in a poem called "To a Friend Whose Work Has Come to Nothing":

> Now all the truth is out,
> Be secret and take defeat
> From any brazen throat,
> For how can you compete,
> Being honour bred, with one
> Who, were it proved he lies,
> Were neither shamed in his own
> Nor in his neighbours' eyes?
> Bred to a harder thing
> Than Triumph, turn away
> And like a laughing string
> Whereon mad fingers play
> Amid a place of stone,
> Be secret and exult,
> Because of all things known
> That is most difficult.

Amazing how Yeats unearthed the theme in the rhyme—"exult" and "difficult." I imagine him strolling the fields of Coole Park and Ballylee, his worn shoes rhythmically rustling the grass that glistened under the slanting Galway sun, as he tuned, in his mind's ear, this sound allegiance. "Exult/Difficult." Poems come not out of intention, but out of surrendering to the felicities of language: what Finn MacCumhal, the mythic Irish hero, calls "the music of what happens."

The difficult thing that Gabriel Conroy must accomplish is to put aside pride, joy, valor, even perhaps tenderness, and exult secretly in deep soul. When I say that writing begins with failure, I mean only that it begins there—what happens next is what counts. Most people give up. I think that those who make writing a life's vocation aren't necessarily the most talented; they are merely the most willing to experience profound and continuous defeat. As W. D. Snodgrass used to say, when asked if someone should become a poet, "Not if they can be happy doing anything else."

The prevailing response to failure is resistance. And our response to that response is also tinged with resistance. As teachers, coaches, parents, bosses, what do we say?

"Try harder,"
"Pick yourself up by your bootstraps,"
"Push, push, push."
"Resist."

Confronted with a specter of adolescent love from long ago, Gabriel doesn't resist. He doesn't rage against his wife or against fate. Instead Joyce tells us that "Generous tears filled Gabriel's eyes." Thinking of Michael Furey's passion, Joyce narrates, "He had never felt like that himself towards any woman, but he knew that such a feeling must be love."

Today, at our graduation from the creative writing program at Wilkes University in the Year of Our Lord Two Thousand and Sixteen, I do not praise resistance. I say we must immerse ourselves in failure. We must drown in failure. We must fail exultantly, extravagantly, repeatedly. As the American poet Paisley Rekdal writes,

> I am going to fail.
> I'm going to fail cartilage and plastic, camera and arrow.
> I'm going to fail binoculars and conjugations,
> all the accompanying musics: I am failing,
> I must fail, I can fail, I have failed
> the way some women throw themselves
> into lover's arms or out trains,
> fingers crossed and skirts billowing
> behind them. . . .

"To succumb, to be destroyed, / to die completely," Rekdal writes. "to fail the way I've failed in every particular sense of myself, / in every new and beautiful light."

Great writing does not aspire to mere success. We cannot write our way into deep soul. There is always a yearning space between our feelings and the alphabet that encodes thought. For me, walking like Gabriel Conroy into the suburbs of old age, the irony is that Gabriel's confession of failure *is* the most refined and intense feeling: his lifelong love for Gretta is far deeper than Michael Furey's youthful passion.

In fact, great writing may not be passionate at all. It may be that for all our pride and joy and valor and tenderness, we create only rough drafts, and it is not until they pass through the phantasmagoria of the revenant that they are fully realized. For all our labors, I'm here to say, at this celebration of success, that writing is not a personal activity, it is a soulful receptivity. Art is the impression left upon the mind when all writing has been effaced.

As darkness falls, Gabriel does not turn toward Dublin's lamplight. He yields his pride, joy, valor, and tenderness to the ghost of Michael Furey standing under a dripping tree. "His soul had approached that region where dwell the vast host of the dead. . . ."

Today, as for Gabriel, the time has come for us to set out on our journey westward. Gabriel's journey takes him toward the wild Atlantic surf, towards his wife's secret past, toward the poor and forgotten and oppressed, toward sleep, toward death. Our journey is a soul-nurturing voyage, one that cannot be forecast or controlled. It demands that we allow every detail and nuance and feature of the world to pass before our eyes, and at the same time allow the chimera to fade to a snowdrift. It requires us to attend, beneath the markings we make on page or screen, to the thrum of sleep, of death, of community, of wonder.

"Yes, the snow was general all over Ireland. It was falling on every part of the dark central plain, on the treeless hills, falling softly upon the Bog of Allen and farther westward, softly falling into the dark mutinous Shannon waves."

Today, on the eve of disaster in our benighted country, I invoke the ghost of Michael Furey to touch us all, softly murmuring every particular note, whispering into being each minute shard, casting every shade and nuance, and at the same time sinking beneath, by the agency of rhythmic utterance, to the powerful unity without which our writing is mere words.

"It was falling too on every part of the lonely churchyard on the hill where Michael Furey lay buried. It lay thickly drifted on the crooked crosses and headstones, on the spears of the little gate, on the barren thorns. His soul swooned slowly as he heard the snow falling faintly through the universe and faintly failing, like the descent of their last end, upon all the living and the dead."

THE WARDEN OF DOVER BEACH

"The sea is calm tonight."

My arms glide over a sea of tranquil desks.

"Arnold opens with a simple statement. The evening's weather report."

I smile at bucolic rows.

"The poet lives seaside—so, 'tonight.'"

Projected text dapples the whiteboard.

"But the next line," my forefinger conducts, "is a musical phrase, introducing the tension between speech and song."

The ceiling fan whirrs.

"So, rhythm."

An ocean of silence.

"Not iambic," I chop pentameter. "And rhymes don't seem to fall regularly." I pointer moony squiggles and recite, "The tide is full; the moon lies fair . . ."

I might as well be on the moon.

"It's dualistic," I peer down at earth. "Sung as measure—two beats, then three, with a strong caesura; or read as a sentence."

From a distant shore, my bluetooth hisses.

"I don't hear it."

"What?" I cup my tinnitus.

"Rhythm," the earbud hisses.

"Sorry?"

"Do Not Hear It, Man," drawls the phantom voice.

"Right," I sigh.

Most of this is happening in my head. Yes, I am in an empty classroom. I am in fact teaching "Dover Beach." And these are the chestnuts I might offer if the auditorium were full: if the back-row sloucher's T-shirt read, "fuck (1)it." If the snapping in my ear was gum chewing. If the watery blue at the back of the room dripped from two hundred glazed eyes.

But it doesn't and they don't. No smart-ass T-shirts here, and gum—along with paper clips, spiral notepads, ink cartridges, the Internet, physical touching, first names, voting, and contraband—is banned.

I am hand-shadowing to a phantom class, hooked up to closed-circuit TV. A screen, wide as a frigate sail, stretches twenty rows away. The monitor switches between two blurry rooms. On the back wall of one room is a barred window. The other room is institutional gray. The figures in the windowed room are male; in the gray room, female. The orange tunics in both rooms are stamped D.O.C. I'm teaching Matthew Arnold to state prisoners.

I myself learned rhythm rocking to Clancy Brother albums, farther from Queens than the Aegean. And farther still—the Latin Mass, where rhythm was flensed of meaning; a dome infused with panoply and incense. Wherever sense is mystified—as in a come-all-ye or church liturgy—the measure is pronounced. In this class, a nineteenth-century pastoral poem rocking with tremulous cadences and turbid ebbs shouldn't lack mystification. Still, the voice in my earbud doesn't hear it.

Do I hear it? Or am I lecturing to myself? "Dover Beach," I've been taught, is literature. It popped up on the Pearson textbook platform, where you choose classics off a menu. The lineup features all the usual suspects from Aeschylus to Eliot. Yes, there is Achebe and Baldwin and Komunyakaa and Walker. I checked those off too. But before I entered this classroom, I didn't know what would be heard—or how. Would incarcerated students want "relevance," considering that what is most relevant is the absence of even the simplest choices: what to eat and wear, and when and where to sleep? Their lives, as they describe them, are most intensely lived in collect phone calls, fritzy TV, scrawled letters, and family visits cowled with uniforms. For attendance in this course, they receive "good days," tiny increments of early release. Why not read nineteenth-century English verse? Why not be mystified by oblique references and antiquated syntax and unfathomable rhythms? At worst, it seems prudent to learn "The Man's" way of talking, so they can recognize him in poems as they heard him, once, in a dread sentence.

Personally, I am unattuned. I included "Dover Beach" almost reflexively, the way one mumbles *eight* counting backward under anesthesia. Maybe these desiccated lines emit some glow. Maybe this chestnut is a talisman or vaccine. Perhaps the arcane diction and elusive references and labyrinthine rhymes might conjure escape.

"Try this trimeter trapdoor."
"Slash with this slant rhyme."
"Clamber up the naked shingles of the world."

But no go. The voice in my ear does not hear it. No challenge. No whine. Not he *won't*. Not he *can't*. His double-barreled spondees: DO NOT HEAR IT, punctuated with the downbeat, "MAAN," concedes no ground. He doesn't lack the faculties to hear what I—The Maan—call rhythm. He *does* not hear it. He does *not*.

Of course no "Man" owns rhythm. It riffs and whirls transformed in every heart and body politic and tribe. One listener hears music; another, tinnitus. Me? In this empty room, I listen. Does a door inside the poem swing open? Do I feel a giddy twinge of the high nonsense? I could wade into these syllables, stripping off significance and context, fay as an aisling, dire as Agnus Dei: *glimmering and vast* in *tremulous cadence.*

Tonight concludes the first line; the second *fair;* then *light* illuminates; but in the fourth line *cliffs stand.* But do they stand when *stand* stands in for *sight* or *might* or *fight* or *tight*—rhymes that might close? I'm standing in a *moon-blanched land.* Where am I being led? *The tranquil bay* beckons a specter—silent, unresolved—*Come to the window, sweet is the night air!"* By whose command? In what signature?

Yet, when I reach toward the moon-blanched screen—silence.

It's not just the screen.

In "site visits," I pass through the checkpoints and am escorted over the court-yard grid to the classroom. Everyone shakes hands. We smile and josh. We take each other in. We are slightly amazed that we are real. But even face to face, we cannot really touch. We cannot wander from the squired paths, or share a meal or evening. I cannot stay one night.

So, I cue up YouTube. Rap rhymes with happening now; there's no *turbid,* no *was once;* no *sound a thought;* no *retreating, to the breath / Of the night wind.*

On the cool blue stage above the orchestra pit, Def Poetry's Mos Def calls out, "Queens, you made it through the metal detectors." Cheers.

"The Bronx, congrats on parole." Louder.

"The Planet of Brooklyyynnnn," the invocation soars and the mic drops and the house explodes.

"Do you hear it now, Bluetooth?"

We are here together. Vibrant, in time. Speaking the self in great rondure and cohesion of all the ring of comrades that HBO pans before zooming on rapt faces going to dissolve. We are here as Georgia Me and Lemon and Black Ice give utterance to this as it is out there and we are all in it together and it flows over and through not like Sophocles and I breeze past rows of desks to touch the screen as Nikki Giovanni takes the stage. Then Rita Dove. Then Baraka. Amiri Baraka. The man himself.

Boo dee da.
Boo dee da.
   Boo dee da.
      Boo dee da. Be do do bee.
         Dee dee dee dee. . . .

What I want is me for real
I want me in myself
   and what that is is what I be
   and what I see and feel and who is me
   and what it is and who it is when it is
   and who it is when it me is what is me
      I'm gonna be here.

The thrum rises; rhythm obtains and prevails; righteous testimony is woven in dream language. This is how Homer sang—to a people entranced from forever to the *now* when we are all together. We *is*. Dover Beach is so far those whiteboard squiggles might be runes.

But it doesn't last. Sound fails. The screen darkens. Gray brick and barred windows reemerge. Everyone is alone. No one is here ourselves.

The army captain who journals about the IED that sent him careening from Kabul to a home that had hardened into drear vast edges—he is not here now. The nurse hospitalized seven times: broken jaw, leg, punctured lung, broken eardrum, all from her husband of whom she writes that it is her daily task to disencumber—she has neither joy, nor love, nor light. The lifer whose son was recently sentenced to life has not certitude nor peace nor help for pain; the daughter who discovered her father's hanging body walks as on a darkling plain.

Are these distances less fraught than Arnold's beach? If rhythm is ebb and flow, if it joins and rejoices, does it not also define, and even exclude? How to explain this estrangement—not just the screen and empty classroom and professorial swagger, but all the pageantry of incarceration: the towers and bandoliers and panopticons. The walkie-talkies and key boxes; the codes; the muting of given names; thrice daily counts; the "Not Fit for Human Consumption" stenciled sacks; the violating frisks; the Abandon All Hope archway; the protocol whereby all visitors surrender cash and electronics and jewelry and license as if entering a medieval airport.

If we fear our neighbors, could it not suffice to attach ankle bracelets and install porch cams? Sentence us home to slum or suburb or prairie or high-rise. If we loathe a portion of ourselves, suffer us primetime. Serve justice on threadbare rugs; thaw Birds Eye; collapse us akimbo in a La-Z-Boy.

It is not fear or loathing only. The orange tunics and frayed drawstrings and rubber soles are not just government issue. They are the habiliments of discord. De-seg and serial numbers and cavity searches are not merely protocols; they are the signifiers of dissonance. The spires and cornices and searchlights, for all their anaphoric power, slur "is" and "us" to Bluetooth hiss.

Do the flickering whiteboard stanzas wall me in? Alone, I sing or pray in vagrant cadences. I draw a rhyme closed or fling it wide. Clancy, Christus, Arnold, and Baraka—the patterns spool and complicate and entwine. But these stanzas framed on whiteboard form a cage.

Why? The canon has no purchase here. There are no quizzes or finals. The text, I tell Bluetooth, is you: what you hear and feel as a poem moves before your eyes or wends into your ear.

No answer. Lines do not speak to my condition or to theirs—only the vastness of the gulf between. On whiteboard, even Baraka's rampant scat-song is mute. Unsung, verses inter measured sound.

"Let us be true to one another," Arnold implores.

Silence. Is anyone there? History says Arnold never lived seaside. There is no love nest, no mistress. There is no Dover Beach, except as Arnold opened a door and waded into *the folds of a great girdle furled.*

No Bluetooth either. I listen to the dark, where solitude is locked in solitary.

Does an unheard rhythm charm the time they serve?

"I'm so angry," said one writer after visiting the empty room.

"What do you mean?"

She looked at me, then at the blurred screen. "Why are these poetry readers in prison?"

At the time, I thought she meant them.

THAT LAMP IS FROM THE TOMB

Tonight I am not going to a movie. I have no Knicks tix. No backstage pass. I will not drift to a séance. Boogey to an orgy. No stumbling to an AA meeting for me. No rendezvous with a dark stranger. Tonight I'm going to a poetry reading.

I love poetry. I have spent my life in its thrall. But tonight I'm going to a poetry reading, and I'm not pleased.

And neither, probably, is the poet. Right now she is wedged in a Longhorn Steakhouse booth between a deanlet and a medievalist. She's nodding and smiling, trying not to blurt, "Shut up, I'm thinking." But no worries. Poets don't prep. They sweat; they panic, but rehearsal? Not so much. In fact, practice just seems so . . . prosaic.

Deep in the mammal brain lurks the notion that the poetry reading should be spontaneous—the public viewing of an ineffable act. The audience can't be there at the moment of composition, when the Muse swoops in, but they can attend this re-creation. So, a junior geezer saunters to the podium, coughs up a joke about Yogi Berra's cellphone, and unfolds an encomium in which the words "risk," "sublime," and "Whitman" figure. I am of course not talking about a particular geezer. Nor a particular poet. I don't even remember who's reading tonight. I'm not complaining about the tall one slouching or the short one vanishing. I'm not calling out the head-bobber, nor the mic popper, nor the dropout from the Charlton Heston acting school. This isn't about the paper shuffling or thumb-licking; not about the digressions longer (and stronger) than the poems themselves. This doesn't have to do with the "I don't know what this poem means because my friends haven't explained it to me yet" or the "I can't say much about this poem except that I was there when it happened." I'm not squeaking about the querulous upticks and appropriated drawls. I'm not even complaining about the "How much time do I have left" black hole, or the way the room's eyes bend to the front row where the geezer's countenance remains regally composed. This isn't even about the "just a few more" routine, and the fingerless math that ensues, everyone dividing the mean length of previous offerings by the cosine "few." It gets dicey. After all, didn't Homer use that ploy?

I'm resigned to all that. Still, I'm not pleased. It's not that I haven't heard some great readings. I've seen Lowell at 92nd Street and Pinsky at Black Oaks and Tess Gallagher at City Lights and Jorie Graham at Prairie Lights. I was at the famous Fort Mason fiasco when Robert Duncan went all Norman Mailer on the Language gang. I've seen Snodgrass play Henry Pussycat and Rothenberg swell to 6'6" and Baraka eviscerate Reagan ("Even Nancy Reagan wouldn't be Nancy Reagan if she could safely be anyone else"). I was there when John Logan did his tribute to The Who, halting midpoem to hurl *The Zigzag Walk* at the amp. I've seen Carolyn Kizer unleash her inner Mae West. And Bill Heyen—who really is 6'6"—called out a backrow yakker with, "You know you don't really have to be here, Sparky."

So, why am I going? To support the poet of course. More—to support poetry. Apparently, poetry needs support. Sales are thin. Grants are down. Outside the NCAA, poetry readings are the only events where the participants don't even get paid. Poetry needs me. So I'm going.

But that's not it, exactly. It's not like supporting Hillary or the Yankees. There's something else. Something just beyond volition. I feel like a child on Sunday morning. Skipping Mass was not an option, after the films of St. Teresa's hell with the flames and squealing animals. Sleeping in was a one-way ticket to Dante-ville. Could it be that I bring a wisp of stale terror to these readings? I thought I shucked God the Father, but even shorn of beard and personhood, he may have infected me with a need for doleful liturgies.

I could go to a slam. Slam poets are funny. They get applause and laughs. They are stand-up comics with no punch lines. It's a cliché to think that some-how this kind of performance is less artistic than literary poetry. Like literary poetry, slam offers an aesthetic experience of language. Like literary poetry, it elevates speech, inviting what William Stafford calls "a certain kind of attention." It differs from literary poetry in its relationship to time, space, and the body. Slam poetry is fully here and now. It involves gesture, movement, even dance. It is choral. It is not less artistic; it is merely more present.

But I'm not going to a slam tonight. I'm going to a reading. And no matter how good, a reading really isn't as much fun as a game or gig or fête or slam be-cause the guest of honor, the star, the big ticket, the emperor of ice cream—that is, the poem itself—has left the building. It is gestured toward, invited, impre-cated, implored. But it is never completely present. It cannot be wholly manifest in performance. It is dense and airy, intimate and elusive. We talk about the mu-sic of poetry, but if there is such a thing it can no longer be heard aloud. It must be seen on the page, refracted from vision to imagined sound, where internal rhymes and enjambed lines and intricate design can be apprehended, and music can be recomposed in the mind's ear.

What a strange event this poetry reading is. It is a staging of what isn't present, except in the hands of the poet: the text. Only she can see the chirography, can follow the line breaks and slant rhymes. She can't render them, except with unnatural pauses or glottal stops or hand signals. But the poet doesn't face the audience: she addresses herself to a fetishized *objet*: the book. Holding the secret symbols, she nevertheless occupies the same position as the audience: she experiences the work as listeners experience it, as if for the first time. In a sense, her reading is a reenactment. The poem is recomposed, and the poet is merely the agent, rather than the cause. The act is multi-dimensional: the reader, the audience, and the text.

After the reading, the triad reconfigures. The poet sits at a table behind a stack of books while the audience lines up to receive benediction in the form of handwriting—a defacement in any other hand is a sacrament when indited by the poet. But more than an autograph, which in the entertainment world provides proof of contemporaneity, the book signing is also a meta-communication. We want not just a signature, but a message. Since most attendees of most readings know the poet personally or share a quasi-professional relationship, the messages vary from the generic "Happy at our meeting" to the supportive, "With hopes for your own work" to the fulsome "Without whom . . ." She may even sketch a graceful glyph, the verse version of an emoticon.

Yes, the reading maps the process: from anointment by the geezer, to anecdote of inspiration, to a reenactment of composition, to the signing which confirms the transubstantiation from utterance to print, and finally to communion with buyers who are named and described in the very hand that composed the poem, reminding us that every book has at least one unfinished page.

Such labor, such panoply. Yet the poem remains at least partly absent. It is as immanent and elusive as another demographic notably missing: the dead. The vast majority of readers are alive, though not all of them seem so. Everyone loves the living. We are so interesting. So full of surprises. And here's a living person willing to share an intimate (if encoded) account of her inner life. A rare chance. Even Language poets have an inner life, and reveal something at a reading, though not necessarily in the poem. Does her text have the qualities of art? Does it reshape the world? Will it outlive its maker? Maybe, maybe not. But the poet is alive, and she speaks and she is interesting to all of us who share her condition.

The dead, like the poem itself, are so achingly near, so desperately far. Their absence is so present. They occupy and do not occupy the empty chairs. They haunt the reading in the form of their poems' ultimate completion, in their facility to render Blake's "place at the bottom of graves where contraries are equally true." In fact, it might be that a poem is merely a draft until it has passed through the breathless presence of the dead.

I suppose the real reason I'm going to a poetry reading tonight, and the reason I'll come home and read poetry, and the reason I'm writing about it, and study it, and teach it, and am forever in its thrall, is because of what it is not. It's not a performance, because it cannot be wholly experienced in one place. No one can follow a poem in one hearing—if you can, it isn't really a poem. Nor can a poem be fully experienced on the page. There's a reason for those thin sales. Reading a novel is a natural, fully satisfying experience (there's absolutely no reason—besides prurience—that I will attend a prose reading. These should be banned completely).

Yet, the page is missing something too. The poetry book is such a poor, bare, forked animal. Sixty-four leaves of solitude: too long for one sitting, too brief for a love affair. Reading poetry alone always makes me feel so alone. Unlike novels, which inhale me, poems never take me out of my body. The acid coffee, the grocery list, the lustful twinge, the provost's schemes, the specter of death—they don't vanish just because my thumb and forefinger are pressed to the spine of Neruda's odes. Reading poetry is disorienting, but not transporting. I feel a strangely present absence, a nostalgia for what never was. Undergraduates, the only members of the general population who read poetry, have a term for this experience. They call it "Bor. Ing."

So, I'm not happy at a reading and I'm not happy reading. Oh my. Does poetry have no native means of apprehension? No presence in the sublunary world? Unlike painting, it cannot be completely appreciated by sight. Unlike music, it is not wholly manifested in sound. In fact, absence is at the heart of poetry. By eluding time and place, it somehow includes the experience of absence. It catalogs everything that happens and does not. Poetry is the finished thing which is incomplete. It requires belief in something beyond itself. God? Get real. Poetry requires a belief that within language, and outside of any particular iteration of language, there are possibilities that can never be attended at one time. They have one foot outside. They are beyond. They are what we used to call the Muse: not a persona, or a Star Wars Force, but a condition, a state of things. It flickers on the page and in the air. It circumnavigates the dead. And so I'm going to a poetry reading tonight.

But I won't be wholly present. My reading will feature silent voices.

Bashō will whisper, "Even in Kyoto / hearing the cuckoo's cry / I long for Kyoto."
Pound will witness commuters dissolving to flower petals.

And Yeats's pince-nez will glitter.

"They have loud music," he'll riff, playing air guitar.

"Hope everyday renewed," miming a slam mic; "And heartier loves," he'll wail and gesture down the tower stairs.

Arm-in-arm Yeats and never-Yeats will stroll. Let them escort me to tonight's reading. Let us be guided by a not-so-distant light.

"That lamp is from the tomb."

ARE LIVES MATTER?

For this essay I have found it necessary to adopt a pseudonym. More, really. A new identity. No, check that. For this essay I find it expedient to erase my current identity, without committing to an alternative.

Outside this essay, I am a middle-class white male, living in the rust belt of Ohio. I am sixty years old, with no particular credentials to address the issues that choke my Facebook feed. I have not been murdered or illegally detained by the police. I have not been raped with a nightstick or sandbagged in the kidneys until I coughed blood. I have not been sleep-deprived or coerced or economically discomfited. No mickeys have been slipped. No dime bags planted. I have not been marginalized. No one in my family has been constrained. My encounters with the U.S. authorities—the public urinations, the busking, the beer heists, the drunk driving, the bar fights, the flag burnings—have all passed harmlessly into the personal mythology of my youth.

I have been permitted to describe my own orbit around the American Culture, which never outside this essay have I called "the American Culture," being so pervasive I had no name for it, as the Greeks had no name for religion, or fish for water.

But an essay from this source may be easily dismissed. It may seem fragile or defensive or microaggressive or triggering. And while I am often defensive, fragile, and macroaggressive, for the purposes of this essay these attributes are counterproductive.

This essay is about privilege. And who wants to read an essay about privilege by a pale-faced junior geezer from Ohio?

I could, of course, pull a Rachel Dolezal, or better, a Yi-Fen Chou, considering that print is more easily darkened than complexion. But I do not want to usurp an identity, just shed my own. For the purposes of this essay, and with the stipulation that outside the purview of this essay I retain all rights and prerogatives to my natal ID—I want to be no one.

I foresee obstacles. First, it will be noted that the ability to shed identity temporarily without loss of rights and prerogatives is by nature a feature of privilege. Second, identity is so deeply inscribed, we suspect any polemic to which a brand does not adhere. Third, most attempts to shed identity merely adopt a new one or evade the question. See George Eliot, Ossian, H. D., A. E., Ai, Christ, Stalin, Prince, Bashō, Captain Kangaroo, and Anonymous.

Yet, hasn't everyone sometimes wanted to be no one? Not just someone else. Truly no one. Dickinson claimed to be nobody. Heine pined not to have been born. Shakespeare went to great lengths to conceal her Irish origins.

The first to try was Odysseus. But even he couldn't pull it off. The strain of self-erasure was so great he had to shout his name to the Cyclops, and you see where that got him.

Maybe nobody can be no one. Maybe we're all locked into who we are. But then, what's the point? If we are all different and separate, and each individual reflects only a single predetermined point of view, why write? Just to validate other white geezers? I guess I could sell to AARP or Rotary. But I don't need the money.

Tentatively, with deference, this essay proposes that somewhere in our core we yearn to believe that all humans are composed of the same stuff, and that in writing we transliterate the desire to address the no one who is both ourselves and others.

Is such yearning fatuous? Solipsistic? Maybe. But really, is it so hard—becoming no one? It's been accomplished by a hundred billion souls and counting. In fact, almost nobody fails to become no one almost immediately following their demise. For the few who linger, what do they retain? They resign nonsalient skills; those who passed before electronics lose voice and movement; those who died before photography lose face. All lose affections. All lose futures. All lose the power of revision—though they themselves continue to be revised.

Those who die without becoming no one comprise a special class. They are called "history" and they are defined entirely by the living. Yet the living are shifty—themselves continually transitioning to no one. In all cases, dead identity is unsustainable. The further back we go, the more it's corrupted—from history to rumor and finally to myth. We know Einstein's hairdo and Mickey Mantle's bourbon. But Daniel Boone? Sappho? Zarathustra?

Whatever achievements, accidents, crimes, or tragedies inspire the preservation of their names, in the ledger of the dead only two features remain permanently indited. The dead retain their gender, and they retain their race.

And this raises a question: not "Do Black Lives Matter?" nor "Do All Lives Matter?" but rather, "Are Lives Matter?" Do they consist of anything but?

So, I've talked myself out of wanting to be no one even within the parameters of this essay. Even though it admits of only two classes—its readers and everyone else—this essay will not argue that it is not a privilege not to be detained without due process. It is not a privilege to be fairly treated in the workplace, or to expect neighbors' respect. It is not a privilege for one's churches to remain unburnt, one's youths unharassed. This essay will not contend that even in the Greeks' religion and the fishes' water these are not privileges but rights. If rights are being denied an entire class of citizens, then this essay will not urge immediate action. This essay will remain silent on civilian review boards and community action committees. It will avoid issues of police militarization and unofficial apartheid. This essay will not decry further study. It will not sneer at heightening awareness. And under no circumstances will this essay revisit the ancestral row house where the Berrigans burned draft cards and Serpico unloaded and Malcolm X and Dr. King were murdered and a napalmed girl screamed through the TV into our Queens living room and I bared my eyeteeth and flailed across the table from my father, an Irish cop, whose eyes rolled back unbelieving because he was only an ocean and a generation from being a Fenian Taig and now we were all nearly Brits ourselves.

This essay will not invoke my father's name, which outside this essay I have inherited, because without that invocation he is no one. And since he is not formally subpoenaed, I can testify that never during those endless battles over the cooling meatloaf did my father utter a vulgarity or cast an aspersion on negroes—that was their name then, no longer colored, not yet people of color—so when the American police rampage in Ferguson and Baltimore and Texas and Staten Island, I exhale hard against the inside of my skin, recalling that after strokes darkened his mind, but before he became no one, my father's impaired tongue spasmed words I had not known he knew, and I fear that beneath the fiction of our identity is not no one, but a vulcanized id, which his tireless will suppressed for seven decades and has now erupted on the streets of America. And what will become of me?

I am becoming old. Soon I will be no one, a transition with no bearing on this essay. But there is no denying that here as everywhere else I am white, though not as white as I once was.

To feel fully white one must be rare, as I was in Zaire, where I was young, American, and definitely white. Despite the flip-flops, beads, and fat-tired bikes, notwithstanding the dreads and wax hollandais and lutuku-binges and the ambling through the *marché*, we *Corps de la Paix* goslings were whiter than we were anywhere else.

Here were our privileges: Less likely to be shot by militaires. More likely to be medevaced if shot. Less likely to be incarcerated. More likely to drink at the Karavia. Less likely to starve. More likely to watch videos at the consulate. Less likely to walk barefoot miles on end. More likely to be instructed to immediately vacate the scene of an accident; less likely to labor; more likely to get paid; less likely to die in infancy; more likely to be importuned by street urchins; less likely to know which interactions were affected by white privilege, or to what degree; more likely to be imperfectly socialized on account of that ignorance; less likely to witness one's family dispersed and village razed and country torn apart by civil war.

But most important: far, far more likely to leave. Not the nightly leave-taking of sleep, nor the final departure which nullifies all privilege. Whiteness entitled us to leave one place to occupy another where the first would still live in memory. When I was most white, everything was a dream I would wake from.

Yet even there I didn't feel completely white. Even though I had to look for confirmation no further than my own reflection, I didn't think, for instance, that departing the Training Center at the Bukavu Institut Superieur Pedagogique to trek a thousand miles by camion to Goma and then by two-night ferry down Lake Tanganyika to catch the sixty-hour train from Kalemie to Lubumbashi where food and job and house and domestique awaited, meant that I was free as few were free—to dream and wake at the same moment, to live that double life where no one counts.

So it did not seem particularly privileged to sneak off the boat in the Tanzanian town of Kigoma without visa or *devise*, armed only with the warning, "Boat leaves at nightfall."

My first day on my own in Africa, I was alone in my own skin and felt at home on earth. I felt and did not feel all eyes following and sensed and did not mind the bodies cresting around me and saw but did not register the round clay huts and the single brick steeple under the sun. I smelled the tang of palm oil-smoked tilapia and waved to the mamas sitting straight legged, weaving baskets, and stopped to watch two men hoisting a skinned python on a pole, while around me the kwashiorkor-bellied *mtotos* chanted "*msungu, msungu*," but this essay will not descend into history. History makes everyone rare. History is how whites colonized Africa. Speke and Burton and Mungo Park and Sir Roger Casement and Conrad all craved to be no one as they traipsed across the continent, scribbling a vibrant landscape into something menacing and dramatic, a setting for self-discovery. They were white, purely white, and that was the point: Only here where everyone else was unwhite could they plumb whiteness. Only here could they chart its features: less likely to act as a group; more likely to make maps; less likely to believe that black lives matter; more likely to regard ahistorical lives as mere matter; less likely to be enslaved; more likely to export; less likely to sleep communally; more likely to use firearms; less likely to uncover their bodies; more likely to contract malaria; far, far, far more likely to leave. No wonder their books sold: their diaries were history, and even though we've glimpsed similar dynamics around the world—Unionist to Catholic, Klansmen to African American, Tutsi to Hutu, Brahmin to Shudra—it was here, in whiteness, that the voyage to no one went farther than it had ever gone before. It meant then and means now living and dreaming at the same moment. It is the ghostly construct where lives are more than matter. History charms us into thinking we are no one while we are still here.

So, purely as exposition and with no pretense to history, this essay will note the shriek of boat whistle at 3:00 p.m. and register my dash to the dock from which the ferry steamed out on the lake toward the Zairian horizon. It will record the sniggering of navvies and the Tanzanian bobby's gap-toothed smile, "Week. Boat comes back in one week."

It is difficult but not impossible to resist history. It requires careful attention to a painful truth. Beneath that week of escapades—the conniving with the Zairian consul and the *sessuin* with the Scottish missionaries and the Bronx cheer to the Benedictine monk and the larking with the boat boys and dickering under the moon with Jean, a *commerçant* who was deep into brokering a deal with diamond smugglers to repatriate me back across the lake by seaplane or motorboat or pirogue—was the purest privilege.

But on the cusp of being no one, there are times when I give in. I close my eyes and feel the wind in my hair and hear the roar of the dilapidated jeep and brace for the next jolt along sunburnt miles, my second-to-last afternoon in Tanzania, heading inland away from the receding lake. And even within the confines of this essay, I fall into history.

"Why?" I asked, but Jean just smiled and waved.

"Why are we going away?"

"You'll know, you'll see," he said.

It didn't matter. We were voyaging together. We were traveling uncharted roads into Africa. One day I would leave, and everything would be transposed.

Finally we stopped, nowhere on the savannah with nothing in sight as far as I could see, and they pointed toward the falling sun where one huge encumbrance heaved grotesquely out of scorched clay: a baobab, whorled in bulbous knots and lichen but bearing its own weight and leaves, alive.

My friends looked and looked, from baobab to me to baobab and finally I asked, "What about the boat?"

"No boat today," Jean shrugged. "Maybe tomorrow."

The baobab might have been holy, they watched so solemnly. We all watched together. Desert birds circled far overhead and I recalled that a *formateur* in Bukavu had told us that the baobab was a phenomenon, because inside its huge heft the trunk was hollow. Alive, it was composed inside entirely of air.

This was their history, I thought. They would reveal it to me and then it would be ours. Standing up in the jeep in the searing African sun living and dreaming at the same time I thought it might belong to me too, and that I would pass on this history long after I left.

"What is the tree?" I asked.

Jean raised his arm and pointed.

"This is Ujiji," he said.

"Yes?"

"That is the baobab."

History says mango but I heard baobab.

"That is the tree where Livingstone met Stanley."

"What?" I spluttered. "Who?"

"Dr. Livingstone, I presume." Jean snapped a mock salute.

I turned from Jean to the great tree and back.

"We came all this way to see Stanley and Livingstone?"

Jean shrugged. "We thought you whites must care about such things."

THIS POEM IS ILLEGAL

In Lak'ech

> *Tú eres mi otro yo.*
> You are my other me.
> *Si te hago daño a ti,*
> If I do harm to you,
> *Me hago daño a mi mismo.*
> I do harm to myself.
> *Si te amo y respeto,*
> If I love and respect you,
> *Me amo y respeto yo.*
> I love and respect myself.

In the state of Arizona, this poem is illegal. Of course, many things in Arizona stretch the law. Leaving your piece at home, for instance, is "Failure to Brandish." Abiding Obama is "The Kenyan Conundrum." Speaking Spanish . . . well that just speaks for itself. But "In Lak'ech" definitely crosses the line. Recitation of this poem in public schools is prohibited by the Arizona Board of Education.

I could saddle up. I could say that Luis Valdez's "In Lak'ech" expresses a sentiment few could contest. It is a powerful and authentic lyric. It is immediate, yet not quite colloquial. Accessible yet mysterious. In its bilingual form, the poem allows monoglots to straddle sound and meaning. They can translate and recompose. The words themselves mean less than the realization that no language is primary. But frankly, despite the fact that the only thing keeping him from committing war crimes is the body fat percentage of Sheriff Joe's posse, I agree with the governor of Arizona. This poem is illegal.

Not the poem itself. On a page or uttered by one voice, it is a sage offering. But poems expand by being shared. They attract meaning not found in the text. As they pass from mouth to mouth, generation to generation, they accrete histories. Clearly, "In Lak'ech" is becoming one weighty utterance. Its power depends on how and where it is recited.

Me? I grew up on the pledge of allegiance and the rosary. At the first bell, sixty citizenlings unfurled from bolted desks, slapped chests, and broke into singsong. For one half minute of homeroom, our whine prevailed.

And the rosary—interminable, but driven by tribal syllabics. Each charm opened with a spondee followed by a slur falling a steep pitch and landing hard on *grace*, from which every scintilla of Queens was flensed, nothing like the bubble-gum "A" of the pledge's *States*. As fingertips rolled beads, the trance grooved till the decade closed on a beveled nut: the patriarchal measure—The Lord's Prayer.

Of course no notion of prosody penetrated. The rites were devoid of attention. That was, I think, the point. Drone by drone, the world was duly relinquished. Slowly we were corkscrewed inside out.

Despite the fact that I sneer at the adulation poured on the pope for express-ing sentiments common to any sophomore (hallelujah against climate change; amen for the poor atheist), still in some synaptic catacomb, I heed no prayer not constructed on poetic principles and not recited in groups larger than three.

I do not think the governor of Arizona and his myrmidons tremble at the power of poetry to alter consciousness. Their level of attention probably matches that of my grammar school classmates. But these days, poetry will take any atten-tion it can get. Getting banned is a coup. Maybe we can even get a schoolteacher to spend a weekend in Maricopa County jail and become poetry's Kim Davis.

Whatever his motives, the guv groks that poems rendered aloud in unison by whole constituencies may ignite changes beyond his control. He might not object to a few hallows and trespasses, but "In Lak'ech" addresses a rival deity. It is a pledge to a foreign power. It is an anti-Anglo spell.

I do not think the governor of Arizona believes in spells, and I share his skep-ticism. The notion that high-falutin' lingo might move God—this we categorically reject. While their origin lies in the nexus between world and word, spells these days are mere literary devices. They showcase language. They are not meant to effect change; they do not appease, entice, or forfend. They are facsimiles. For one thing, literary spells are produced and spoken by a single voter. And only a few times, in odd hours, in unfrequented venues. When a poet—say, Catullus—prays, "only that the gods cure me of this disease / and as I once was whole, make me now whole again," he is not really praying. His audience is not the Olympians, or even humanity—just his literary friends. His prayer isn't reverence, it's style. It's *his* style—meant to render his psychological state at a particular time. This may be the quality that differentiates poetry from prayer, or pledge, or rock lyric, or chant. A poem is designed to be apprehended by one consumer at a time. Try reciting "Howl" in chorus, or even "The Red Wheelbarrow."

"Poetry," Auden famously pronounced, "makes nothing happen." At first glance, Auden appears to endorse discourse over action. He privileges the word over the world. But viewed from another angle, Auden's proposition is dynamic: poetry is not merely passive; it prevents "something" from being the only thing that occurs, and opens a plethora of potentialities. It makes nothing HAPPEN. Auden endows poetry with a power equivalent to mathematical zero.

I do not know if the governor of Arizona is a savvy politician. He did get elected, so he can't be clueless. Still, if I were to advise him in my capacity as an eastern liberal poetry geek, I would counsel him to pivot, and allow "In Lak'ech" to be recited in public schools. Better, I would urge that he make such recitation mandatory—not to support the sentiment, or bilingualism, or the erosion of American values, or the collapse of manifest destiny, but because if poetry gains momentum with headcount, so its efficacy diminishes at a certain critical mass. The cadences which nurtured eventually kill. As phrases that once encapsulated identities and aspirations decay into rote syllables, poetry gets engulfed by the institutions it feeds on.

Stripped of awe, the Hail Mary's "at the hour of our death," becomes comfortably collective. They preach "our" death—an event which, barring redneck apocalypse—is fictional. Real death is always "mine" not "ours."

Detached from civil strife, the pledge's "indivisible" dissolves in a sibilant cloud of smoke. This explains why, even after thousands of recitations of pledge and rosary, I am neither patriot nor Catholic.

I would recommend that the governor take a page from that canny political operative Plato and monitor those poems which resist institutionalization. These are the real subversives. They employ guerrilla tactics, striking from safe houses fronting as libraries and cafes. Their code is unbreakable because it constantly shifts: one poem uses arcane diction, another hendecasyllabics. A third frames a swath of silence. Poems require almost no fiscal support, no supply lines. They don't even need print. For the present they are the desperate weapon of a lunatic fringe. But who knows? The governor of Arizona may one day find himself out-lingualed.

I recommend that the governor send undercover agents to infiltrate a cell. Observe poets in their habitat. Consider these versifiers' commitment to their make-believe regime. There is no coughing or foot shuffling, despite the speaker's amateurism. No one checks their iPhones. The poet has no band, or bunting, or teleprompter. She appears to be reading from a slim paperback or, even more simply, from a loose-leaf binder. Even though she has exhausted her time allotment, even though spines ache in metal chairs and espresso machines snore, even though no one can follow the elliptical spin of her lyric, the small room is rapt, as if listening for an answer to a prayer.

KITH & KIN

I hit my head. Whacked it good. I was parked in a Hertz garage, and as I squeezed out of the compact rental—pow—my skull smacked concrete: bald to wall. Next thing I remember is a hospital bed with a doctor leaning over me.

"What happened?" I slurred.

"Concussion," said the doctor. "How do you feel?"

"Ok, I guess." I fingered the lump. "A bit touched."

The doctor checked his clipboard.

"Who's the president?" he asked.

"Barack Obama."

The doctor frowned.

"What pet meme just went viral?"

"Dogs playing poker?"

He scribbled.

"What campus demonstration is trending?"

"The Big Chill?"

His eyebrows went up.

"What's your Twitter handle?"

"Bluebird?"

"Ok," he unclicked his pen. "We're going to run further tests, but I think that your hypofalsus," he tapped my left temple, "has been compromised."

"Is it serious?"

"The hypofalsus governs a very specific part of brain activity," he said. "It processes short-term secondhand experience—anything immediate that you learn about but don't apprehend firsthand.

"Sounds bad."

"Eh," he shrugged. "There's still a lot we don't know." His palm drifted upward. "Why the hypofalsus doesn't affect nuanced argument, or noncommercial verse, or anything painted by hand, or published in a limited edition, or performed in a minor key."

The doctor shook his head.

"There's been a sharp spike in incidents," he said. "It's not uncommon to see ruptures or even infarction independent of any external trauma."

"I feel OK, Doc."

"The FDA is useless." He wiped his specs. "But the NEJM targets one cause: social media. Blogs, tweets, I.M.s, texts, and YouTube vids cause inflammation. In your case, the last eighteen months of Internet activity has been wiped clean."

"Will I recover?"

"We can't say if the hypofalsus will ever be fully restored—or as we say, 're-storied.' But you can drive, work, operate machinery. There should be no effect on your daily life, except that you may find yourself confused at rallies."

He scratched out a prescription. "No more than twenty minutes a day on Facebook."

Pulling the curtain, he shot back, "And stay off Fox."

In the first weeks after the accident, a lot changed. The world no longer streamed through my devices. All my links were broken. I was unplugged.

When someone mentioned ISIS, I nodded and smiled. Benghazi e-mail scandal drew a blank. I didn't know where Ferguson was, or why Baltimore burned, or what "I Can't Breathe" meant. It was disconcerting. Could cucumbers scare cats? Ice buckets cure ALS? Was Donald Trump really president?

Then there was my own small quadrant of the noosphere—the lit racket. In po-biz, rumors swirled. A lawyer tweeted *Gone with the Wind* as conceptual art; a white guy masqueraded as Chinese to get into *BAP*; an L.A. editor did a walk of shame after a failed joke about cowboys and Indians.

Mostly, it's the police. Everywhere cops were armed and dangerous. I could remember Rodney King and the '68 Chicago Convention. I remembered Serpico and Alabama's Bloody Sunday. It's not as if my hypofalsus had been erased back to Officer Joe Bolton and The Stooges' *Fun House*. But now, police violence had gone viral. Could it be that all over the country blue uniforms were hunting black civilians?

As my hypofalsus started to recover, my head was getting worse. My brain pulsed with pixelated batons, barricades, gas masks, Bluto-vests. It got so bad, I went back to the hospital for a follow-up.

"Doc," I said, "I'm not sure I even want a hypofalsus. I might be better off reading no screen beyond my bedroom window. Is there a pill or something I can take to kill it for good—like thyroid medicine. Or you could cut. Lobotomize. Take it out."

The doctor shook his head.

"We get that a lot these days. And frankly," one hand cupped his mouth, "There are a few quacks out there. But the hypofalsus serves an essential function. It sustains the therapeutic illusion that beyond us, out there," he thumbed the curtain, "is another body—composed of knowledge: a single corpus that we all aspire to attain. When Plato talked about ideal forms—he was using his hypofalsus. The Talmud, *City of God, Communist Manifesto*, e=*mc*² . . ." the doctor spread his arms. "Einstein's brain was hyper-hypofalsian."

"I can't sleep, Doc." I grabbed his wrist. "The world is spinning before my eyes. I can't tell big from small or near from far. My tinnitus is starting to sound like newscasts."

"It's mysterious, the hypofalsus, and nowadays often overstimulated," he said. "Sometimes it gets so hyperactive that the body of knowledge starts to calcify. People hallucinate—think they actually see it. And of course that descends into orthodoxy. Then doctrine. Acronyms. Slogans. It's epidemic.

"But before jumbotrons and quadrophonics, life was easier on the hypofalsus. The brain could distinguish between first- and secondhand knowledge. The page, the scroll, the spoken story were natural filters. Even black and white tubes. But now . . ." his voice trailed off.

"Your hypofalsus needs complete rest. In time, the membrane between the two vectors will strengthen." The doctor's pen squiggled. "Meanwhile, we're going to try a diet of high artifice. Give the hypofalsus a chance to read between the lines. I'm recommending nothing contemporary. Homer, Dante—in the original if possible. Milton is good, and Pound, or Hart Crane, or Zukovsky if your system can tolerate him. Novels are iffy. Joyce, Woolf, Pynchon are nice. Plenty of the higher nonsense. But stay away from Hemingway and Oates."

It's been two months now, and I haven't done well. More and more I dream about life without a hypofalsus. There would be no gun lobby. No right-to-lifers. No killer cops or provosts. Everybody composts. Poetry pays. And there are only two races: kith and kin.

In the unhypofalsified world, kith is a race composed wholly of people I know. I made a mental list. Fifty-six kith. Not all are present, or alive. Some I have not seen for years. Some live in whereabouts unknown. But I know them all.

Color, gender, and ethnicity don't count. Each kith belongs. Each is distinct. Their words and actions form patterns I have experienced. No matter how briefly, or how long ago, each kith has shared a moment with me and we harken to that touch. Most important, kith can be remembered without prompting. Without a functioning hypofalsus, I can't rely on Facebook friends, Twitter followers, gamers, civic club members. I do not scroll or click. I do not like.

My injury has rendered me 92 percent solipsistic, so it doesn't matter that no one but me knows that they are kith. They have no common customs or allegiances or culture or even secret handshakes. They do not necessarily know each other's names. They are a nation only in the sense that Leopold Bloom (who does not qualify because of his fictional status) defines nations: people living in same time and place, or not. Of course Bloom's definition was limited by three thousand years of tradition. As a solipsist, I lack that inhibition.

I do not count the newly born, even infants born to kith. Without a nametag or mascot bib, I could not recognize them till they learn to speak. Not that speech is the determining factor. There are many kith with whom I have held little conversation. But newborns, no. Still, excluding the unweaned may be mere prejudice. I may be bigoted against babies—their failure to speak or excrete fastidiously or even move more than a few inches should not be held against them, and certainly if a kith lost those faculties—as a few, in fact, have—they would not be exiled. So why should newborns be excluded? I don't know, but I can't help myself. That's the way bigotry is.

Kith is not blood. I have excluded cousins. Kith is not people I like. The kith sports a few pricks and shrews and two ninety-proof assholes. There are people I love who are not kith. Kith are species-specific. Though I know some animals as well as I know any human beings, my cat is not kith, even when my hypofalsus purrs.

I have made another mental list. People I forgot I knew. This list is completely integrated with kith. I regret the omission, but it's important that I don't crib from premade lists to construct some comprehensive census. List-writing is processed by the hypofalsus. Women slept with. Events of shame. Vegetables. Bar jokes. Best-ofs. If items don't live in memory, they aren't part of an unfalsified life.

My second counting yielded fifty-three new kith, and it also complicated matters. For instance, what about people who've had a big effect, but whom I can't really claim to know—nuns and professors and cops and priests and doctors—including the doctor who diagnosed my hypofalsus. They are terribly important, and yet do I know them? I have identified thirty-seven people in addition to the 103 listed so far who fall into this category. I'm undecided about their status.

And what about famous people? Not celebrities, who are clearly excluded on the grounds that I experience them only by the agency of a healthy hypofalsus. So, in my condition, I do not experience them as people at all. But people I have studied: writers and historical figures whose work has affected me?

I've decided that the kith, in order to function, must exclude these worthies, though I feel like Dante excluding Homer and Virgil from Paradise.

Some kith are privileged. Others are oppressed—by color or gender or age discrimination, by impending mortality or past tragedy. A few belong to the most downtrodden: the dim and homely—populations so despised that slurs against them are socially acceptable.

Roughly, kith demographics are as follows: 72 percent Caucasian; 80 percent U. S. citizens; 43 percent female. Mean age forty-seven. Median income undetermined, but some estimates place at 672 percent of global mean. And me? 90th percentile of age; 82nd percentile of education; 29th of integrity; 71st athleticism; 42nd life expectancy; 91st of height; and 50th of likability.

I'm OK with those numbers.

But still, I'm left with everyone else. If googling didn't frazzle my hypofalsus, I'd get a nose count. As it is, there is a whole planet of people I don't know. These are the kin.

For a week or two, the kin seemed all the same. It wasn't that they looked or acted alike. It wasn't that they seemed familiar, or friendly, or even comprehensible. It just didn't matter. Everyone was kin, which is true, genetically speaking. Any one of them could have stepped forward from anywhere and been welcome into kith.

But as my hypofalsus started to itch and tingle, things fell apart. There were kin I didn't know yet but whom I might feasibly encounter; there were kin who spoke my language or a cognate; kin who played sports I played or ate appetizing foods. There were kin whose customs I knew from living in their countries.

Others I had no idea about: the Iroquois and the Tibetan, the Aboriginal and Portlandian. But somehow the ones I knew seemed farther away than the ones I could barely imagine. I knew how little I knew of the groups I knew. As my hypofalsus healed, calling them all kin seemed impossible. Religion, color, dress, language, cheekbones, political and economic systems, utensils, art, modes of transportation, climate—everything near and far—started to splinter. Everyone spun farther and farther away from everyone else, and away from me.

What about terrorists who wanted to kill me without knowing me? What about the aged who didn't even know themselves? The malnourished, the mentally ill, the cufflink wearers and machete wielders? What about the a cappella singers? Were there kin in the vanishing rainforests? Beneath melting icecaps? Deans' offices? What of legions dying in American prisons? Were they kin too?

The doctor says that my problem may not be my recovering hypofalsus. Other parts of the brain, he says, may be compensating, the way the blind become more sensitive to sound.

But walking the streets at night I'm lost and inconsolable. Who are my kin—the passersby? The faceless cabbies and truckdrivers? The joggers, bikers, polemicists, dog walkers, hipsters, lummoxes, and models gliding up and down the city avenue? I want to accost everyone.

"Tell me your story," I want to beg. "By what cause were you conceived? How did your ancestors wend here? What's behind your glasses? How did you appear before my eyes?"

I babble, gesture, and mutter to myself. I would grope strangers, stop traffic, wave and dance at stoplights to understand why kin seem every day a little more unkind. Only fear of the police restrains me. I'm afraid some cop with a fried hypofalsus might not realize I am white.

I know my problem is not new. The hypofalsus has driven better people mad. Look at Oedipus—he lived by the hypofalsus, peering straight at the body of knowledge. He named the body "Sphinx" and he solved it. Race hatred, abuse, oppression—he had them all figured out right up to the moment he didn't. That's what the hypofalsus does: makes you think you know right up to the instant that you don't. Stabbing knitting needles into his eyes—it wasn't that Oedipus didn't want to see. He loved his children. He hugged them underneath the hanging body of his mother-wife. It wasn't that he wanted to go blind. He would have died to lay eyes on his dead father. He still wanted to see whatever faced him. It wasn't his eyes those needles were aimed for. I know. It was his pulsing, quivering hypofalsus.

PART
3

LINE & SENTENCE

JACK

Escorting me from Queens to Lewisburg, the Bradys sailed across the Delaware Water Gap, farther west than we had ever been. Past the frontier, we pulled over at a rest stop off Route 80. Father poked my kid brother awake. Mother slipped out of the back seat. In the parking lot, truckers dozed in giant cabs. Grown-ups of uncommon girth swatted offspring into the brick pillbox. Large birds pecked trash. We did our business and set out again. Twenty miles later, Father turned to the backseat, "How much further, Pet." Silence. We had left Mother at the rest stop. That's how bad I wanted and feared college.

What did I want and fear? First kiss. First toke. First wrought iron gate. First 6'7" opponent. First assignment. First adult repartee. But most, first Professor— that is, first Virgil lighting the dark way.

I got the class and game and frat and girls' dorm—and they were worth it. What I'm still getting is the Virgil.

I'm still getting Professor Carens chattering back to *Ulysses*. Ineluctable modality of the visible? No clue. *Liliata rutilantium te confessorum turma circumdet? Pas de chance.* But he got it. I got that he got it, and that one day I might.

I'm getting Professor Payne who listened with a straight face while a Phi Gam theorized that *The Four Zoas* was about football. The class hushed. Blake blanched. But Prof Payne pranced a broken field between Harold Bloom and Howard Cosell. So I thought one day I might run.

I'm getting the ache in Professor Murphy's Saturday morning forehand, and the tuneful wail of Professor Taylor's fiddle, and the sheepish grin as Professor Reese paged an old grade book that recorded, next to Roth, Philip: "C+."

I'm getting age. Mortality. I'm getting that when Visiting Professor Snodgrass said, "Donald Hall is the only poet to learn from Whitman," and "We know now that Delmore Schwartz wasn't a poet," he wasn't pronouncing eternal judgment. He was just sailing in the dark. Maybe, I thought, I too might sail someday.

The one who sailed farthest was the only one who wasn't called "Professor," though he'd earned the title. He was far from no one. He had published books which I had read with the eerie sensation of being on the same grounds as a poet, when I'd thought all poets were dead or at least distant. But here were the books, bound and colophoned; here was the poet walking down the hall of Vaughan Lit to our first class.

For three mortal hours, this living poet sailed through the history of English poetry from Beowulf to Eliot, occasionally pausing to apologize for talking for so long. It was amazing for its brilliance, but more for the fact that he didn't seem to care about brilliance, only about the poems, as if the authors passed outside the window where he set his gaze. It was his history. Someday maybe mine.

In mid-confab, some feathery-bearded gosling raised his hand. I don't recall the question. Only the address, "Jack." The poet looked up—his attention unseated from George Herbert. But there was no lightning bolt. No tweaked dignity. Just "Jack."

It was not a word he taught. I do not know its source. Professor Wheatcroft was not overly familiar or informal or comradely or young. But I got it. I'm still getting it. Although we were at wildly different places, different statures and potentials, although we could never claim his eminence, we were all sailing the same way into the dark. No keystone Virgil here, just Odysseus.

The rest of that magical last term was unscripted. Professor Wheatcroft attended to us in the same manner as he attended to Herbert, Dickinson, and Wilbur. We were present in the same condition. Sometimes he might say something like, "Poets are the physicists of language." Or "It's more important to read than to write." Maybe he said these things, maybe not. It was long ago. Yet, one thing for sure. Rhythmic utterance requires measure and measure requires freedom and freedom requires silence of the quality that Jack Wheatcroft brought into the room. Jack was a poet and the teaching he loved was an analogy for his own sense of making things out of silence, and the silence was sustained with and by the language that we hear in all his varied poems—extraordinarily prolific, but each poem crafted as if it were the first poem.

And it goes on. I never found Virgil, but I learned about ineluctable modality and wound up co-editing a book on Joyce with Professor James F. Carens, now deceased. I listened hard to Professor Jack Wheatcroft's words and silences, and wound up publishing his Selected Poems, *Fugitive Self.*

And after all, I still recross that gap. The Bradys did turn back to pick up my mother on Route 80. Some days I linger at that rest stop, embracing her like Anticlea's ghost.

AUTHENTICITÉ

It's green. Fern, myrtle, chartreuse, Platonic-Kelly. Shamrock-on-steroids. And it's everywhere: derbies, balloons, twirlers, buttons, sneakers, bunting, vests, glitter, boutonnières, smoke. On the limelit stage, the band cranks up. The lead singer sports spiky hair and a harlequin kilt. The tin whistler's jeans are spray-painted K.M.R.I.A. (he must be the English major—it's Joycean for "Kiss My Royal Irish Arse"). Tonight is the high holy moneymaker and they're making the most of it, crooning and ululating and diddlydydaying. Right now they're deep into a *Guinness Book*–length medley of *It's No Nay Ireland Says The Wild Colonial Unicorn's Galway Danny Where It's a Long Way to Mother Macree and Has Anybody Here Seen My Wild Irish Rose*—nuggets of such dreck they must have spilled out of a date-expired box of Lucky Charms. The emerald mob con-geals to climax, chorusing that old Irish tune, Gilligan's Island. Wild applause.

Did anybody ever think any of this was good? Were any of these tunes once hummed on an April afternoon by a gossoon hiking the twelve miles from Ca-van town on the road to Killeshandra? If so, by what process were they strained of flavor and nuance, and injected, like the flu, into the aesthetic arteries of an entire population? If this sexless bacchanalia represents an invocation, what is it calling for? If it's a ritual, what does it reenact? What is it we yearn for?

Right now I can relate to one particular yearning—to be anywhere else. Maybe that's how it begins. Growing up in Queens, which my parents pro-nounced "Galway," our theme song was "Everybody Knows This Is Nowhere." The row houses, the triple-digited streets, the plastic Pegasus gas stations, the unpithed hearts and TV dinners, seemed proof that only by fictive flight could we propel ourselves toward a home that was not completely sanitized of meaning. For me, that fantasy came to life one Saturday morning as I thumbed through the remainder rack of LPs in Korvettes emporium. Amid the mind-blowing covers of Iron Butterfly, Procol Harum, and Jethro Tull was an album featuring four men in white sweaters in front of a canvas backdrop. There it was, the place I didn't come from, where I wasn't born and raised, where I knew no one: home.

I wedged that LP into the cabinet hi-fi and played it raw. Afternoons at a time, I rocked on hands and haunches, back and forth, speed adjusted to song.

Father rolled his eyes. "Up the Rebels."

Mother hissed back, "Narrowback!"

With money shaved from lunch, I collected the entire Clancy Brothers and Tommy Makem catalog, *Hearty & Hellish!*; *Isn't It Grand, Boys*; *The Boys Won't Leave the Girls Alone*; *The First Hurrah!*: *Home Boys Home*; along with Paddy Noonan, The Dubliners, The Irish Rovers, The Merry Ploughboys.

I listened so hard I believed I understood the words: *moonshine, porter, poteen,* and *Sassenach* made sense. I was *langers; peelers, pishogues, and fenians harried and cocked*; I *roved*; I *stood and delivered—a bloody briny daft shoneen* with an eye peeled for a *crubeen* or a *colleen*, a *dragoon*, an *omadon*, a *quay*.

Soon I began to understand Gaelic and *ad fiason la port laragot, fa dow, fa dee, fa le god-e-lum* was clear to me as *with houls ime shoos ame tows peepin troo siyin shinnymarinkadootaloffin ould jonny doo.*

In third grade, I became the ambassador of fantasy—plucked by Sister Miriam Eileen out of the back row and ushered into the sixth grade to preen like an exotic bird and croak "O'Donnell Abu" to the apprentice thugs and prom queens. Though I hewed strictly to routine, walking straight home after school to boil franks with Dinty Moore and watch *Speed Racer*, I lived in a phantasmagoria of faeries, warriors, wild geese, turf fires, and bathos. I mimed step dances. I named our dog "Wolfe Tone." I said Gaelic Mass in my bedroom with a tissue box tabernacle and bathrobe vestments while Wolfe served as acolyte. My mother thought I'd had a stroke when she saw my fourth-grade school picture, because I'd curled my lip in what I took for an Irish smile. Life sailed on between Innisfree and Flushing until fifth grade when the Masterson twins from Limerick enrolled. If they looked like a pair of snivelers who didn't know a bunt from a burrito, they were certifiably more Irish than I was. I never got the nerve even to say hello.

The desire to be somewhere authentic without moving isn't limited to children, or once-a-year-Paddies, or the denizens of faceless suburbs. I've seen a whole country overwhelmed. The flag was green there too—olive drab, with a jaundiced circle into which a black arm thrusts a torch. Painted on walls, flying above office buildings, stenciled on T-shirts, it was omnipresent. Where you didn't see the pennant, you saw the portrait of the man behind it, wearing a leopard skin hat and gripping a tribal staff. He'd changed his name from Joseph Mobutu to Mobutu Sese Seko Kuku Ngbendu Wa Za Banga (Mobutu, He Himself, the Cock That Fears No One). He was President for Life and Father of the Nation. When the Katanga province revolted, he renamed it Shaba. He transformed his native village into an animist shrine. He rechristened the entire country, thwarting cartographers by erasing the Congo on account of its colonial taint, in favor of Zaire, a word with no definitive history—though some said it came from a Portuguese mispronunciation of the Congolese word for "river." He forbad cravats, preferring Nehru-style *abacosts*. Political rallies featured drumbeat-driven dances performed by women wearing *pagnes* silk-screened with the leader's portrait. *Authenticité*, he called it, implying that the war-torn, impoverished country which the "Zairois" experienced every day was merely a façade. If Mobutu's vision was a figment, it was less elusive than his nation's bounty, sequestered in the president's Swiss bank account.

While *authenticité* usually tints the present through the lens of a monochromatic past, sometimes it peers into the future. Describing communist Czechoslovakia, Milan Kundera links programmatic political thought with a cultural aesthetic he calls "kitsch." Kundera's kitsch results from an effort to cleanse; it is, as he says, "the absolute denial of shit." Every institution has its kitsch, he contends: there's communist kitsch and capitalist kitsch and Christian kitsch and even perhaps Buddhist kitsch.

Kitsch, or *authenticité*, or merely sentimentality: all renounce the messy, the frayed, the unclean. But I wonder if there isn't more. Maybe the desire for *authenticité* emerges from dissatisfaction with the here and now—that prison from which none escape, and from which we seem eternally excluded. When the kaleidoscope of this absent-present makes us dizzy, we shut our eyes and envision some Edenic past or utopian future, even though the squint turns everything green or red. Depending on how you spin the palette, it's not that far perhaps from Queens to Zaire to the Communist bloc to the *authenticité* of the Third Reich or Trump's America where demagogues have rallied millions in the name of a fantastic past and future.

Easy now, boy. Take a sip. I can't get all wound up. After all, I'm not merely a spectator here at this St. Patrick's Day free-for-all in Youngstown, Ohio—itself a Hittite anagram for "nowhere." My band's up next.

Yes, despite the Masterson setback, I find myself propped once again in front of overgrown sixth graders to flog the ould songs. We've been at it for years, and it's great *craic*. Living rooms, bars, churches, auditoriums, parking lots, theatres, and festivals: we've hit all the hot spots of northeast Ohio and even beyond—not to mention spiking the occasional moribund faculty tea. But tonight's different. After watching the warm-up crew cudgel the crowd into a frenzy, my bandmates eye me warily. It won't be original ballads or poems set to music or jazzed up arrangements tonight—not with this crowd, not on your life. Nothing but schlock will do. And I'm a veritable jukebox of schlock.

The prospect of reliving my own version of *authenticité* highlights the contrast between tonight's gig and the tunes we play on any of the other 364. In fact, sometimes I wonder if we're an Irish band at all. My fellow band members come from different angles altogether. There's Jim Andrews, a physicist; Kelly Bancroft, a playwright; and Istvan Homner, a Transylvanian mandolin player. Not a green strand in the helix. And what about our long-haired musical leader and composer, Steve Reese, who also "digs with the other foot," as they say in Queens?

When I imagine Steve Reese's childhood, I think of a different kind of *authenticité* altogether. He grew up in Ithaca, in the Finger Lakes district of upstate New York: a hamlet, as it appears from the greenish distance of time and envy, of steeples, ivy, antique shops and cafes. Set in a valley between two campuses, it is replete with presentness, nearly living up to its Homeric etymology as a byword for home. While I was busing around meadowless Fresh Meadows, waterless Bayside and dystopian Utopia, Steve Reese biked home from his red-bricked, white-columned schoolhouse down Cayuga Street, named after the local Indians, onto Willow Ave, lined with real willows. Arriving at a home that must have been Dutch Colonial, he too was immersed in music. But there was no autistic bobbing on threadbare carpet (a practice which, by the way, has had the collateral effect of fitting me perfectly for the bodhrán). Instead, Steve Reese learned to play a guitar his brother had handcrafted. The Reese brothers hunched over reel-to-reel recordings of James Taylor, Bob Dylan, Joan Baez, and a thousand other troubadours, slowing the tape down to amplify each lick until they had absorbed a quadrant of the airwaves. Reese honed his gift playing in country and rock bands while grinding out an Eng. Lit. PhD at the University of Delaware, where by strange fortune, our paths almost crossed—Steve arriving just after I lit out from Blue Hen country for Zaire and *authenticité*.

Late at night, buttery with whiskey, our rehearsals often melt into a songfest from those days, as Steve rocks through unholy medleys—everything from "Take a Letter Maria" to "The Inessential Woody Guthrie" to "Dead Skunk in the Middle of the Road." He has a chunk of Americana by heart, making up for everything I missed.

His solo album, *The Feast of St. Monday,* is an eclectic blend of ballads and alternative rock. Reese's homemade guitar speaks like a lucid voice, textured with fiddle, bass, and drums, and there's not a song on the CD whose lyrics wouldn't stand on their own as spoken poetry. But as much as I love *The Feast of St. Monday*, the work he's done with the band is, for me, the thing I can't account for.

It's wildly inauthentic. Reese clamps some electric chords on James Clarence

Mangan's "Rest Only in the Grave" with enough juice to jolt J. C.'s liver back to life, and restore bits of Davis and Ferguson too.

More ambitious still, "Heart of the Stranger" draws from Walt Whitman's *Specimen Days* to relive an encounter with an Irish soldier who came to America "to fight for Lincoln in '63." Midway through, the melody yields to a spoken stanza of Whitman's "Reconciliation," mediating song and speech, documentation and interpretation. Because the Whitmanesque refrain, "Little he knew, poor death-stricken boy, / The heart of the stranger that hovered near," reveals the sensibility embodied in all these songs, *Heart of the Stranger* became the title of our second CD.

Another composition mixes the structure of a contemporary alternative song, including bridge, refrains, harmonies, and dueling instrumental breaks, with lyrics that echo the testimonial narratives of nineteenth-century sheet ballads. The result brings to life the voice of a woman about to board one of the infamous famine ships.

> In the end we'd grown desperate,
> Having for our only meal,
> A handful of Peel's brimstone,
> And whatever we could steal.
>
> My husband left us at the workhouse door,
> And the child growing weak,
> I staggered the road down to Dublin,
> The famine ships to seek.

Unable to extinguish his academic instincts, Prof. Reese has nosed through many volumes to uncover elements that seldom reach contemporary ballads. Peel's brimstone, for instance, refers to the indigestible grain that Sir Robert "Orange" Peel imported to feed the starving Irish. Likewise, Reese links nodes of oppression, observing that "The boat smelled of sugar and molasses / From its West Indies port of call." Personal and immediate, the suffering evoked by "Famine Ship" ripples far beyond national borders.

Then there's the blues number laid on the fourteenth-century Welsh poet, Dafydd ap Gwilym. Opening with a bass riff that Dafydd's musical descendant, Muddy Waters, might have jammed, Reese wails,

> A plague upon the women of this parish.
> What's wrong that they don't want me.
> Not just the girls, but the wives and widows.
> It's unnatural; it's villainy.

"Dafydd's Lament" moderates a quarrel between the poet and his accusers, who respond in a lighter modality, "To lie between a maiden's legs is the one thing on his mind. / In his eyes the fire of lust is all that you will find." When the women finish flaying the arse off him, the instrumentals descend back into the blues to preface the next chapter from the aging poet.

The inventiveness of this hybrid becomes more apparent if we peek backstage at some sources. Here's a sample, translated in *The Celtic Poets*.

> Furious and indignant am I!
> A plague on the women of this parish,
> For I never had one of them, ever
> Nothing but failed endeavor,
> Not a prayer with a tender maid,
> Nor girl, or wife or hag!

Not hard to see the grain Reese works against: the stilted "furious," "indignant," "endeavor," and "never had I one." Yet, in unvarnishing Dafydd's lust, Reese hasn't merely sanded down the diction; this is no Beat version. "Plague," "parish," "unnatural," and most delicious of all, "villainy," ink the colloquial lines with a kind of medieval slang.

Unlike the first-person lyric format of the translations in *The Celtic Poets*, "Dafydd's Lament" reframes an ancient practice: the poetic contest. Such sparring tournaments have ancient roots; they provide the template for Oedipus's riddling; and they appear in many medieval poems, perhaps most famously in Brian Merriman's bawdy *The Midnight Court*, where early feminists put the male gender on trial, deciding we come up (cough) short. Such contests are frequently featured in rap, and "Dafydd's Lament" incorporates a strand of this genre by devolving into a spoken brawl: "Look at him with his oily eyes; more white hair than my grandmother," say the women—to which the poet can only pluck a G and splutter, "Oh, it's unnatural."

Reese digs further back into the canon to give voice to "The Old Woman of Beare," an anonymous eighth-century Irish poem. Again, it's instructive to see the material from which his lyrics are culled. Here's a stanza from *The Faber Book of Irish Verse*.

> Ebb tide has come for me:
> My life drifts downwards
> Like a retreating sea
> With no tidal turn.

This postmodernist translation bends the slant rhymes of Gaelic verse into jagged lines. Reese takes the simple tone, along with more fulsome treatments by Frank O'Connor and Kuno Meyer, and gives the poem a new spin, based on a three-four time signature that syncopates accented and slant rhymes against a complex melodic pattern.

> The sea it crawls away from shore,
> Leaves weeds like a corpse's hair.
> That desolate, withdrawing sea is in me,
> I'm the old woman of Beare . . .

Of course, exegesis can't convey the pleasure of sitting around my living room, as we did last night, encircled by vocal harmonies, guitar, mandolin, bass, and bodhrán, knowing that this place in rainy March in Ohio is the only spot on earth where this eighth-century poem is being played in the spirit that ensorcelled the wind-wracked Beare Peninsula twelve hundred years ago. Last night, it felt palpable: the tensile strength that comes from the melding of influences.

One characteristic of genuine folk music (meaning anything that's been loved so deeply by so many that the names have rubbed off) is that there's not much skin between the living and the dead. Just as Reese writes in the voice of an eighth-century crone, or a homeless drunk, or a great American Civil War poet, so the tradition glides over ephemeral distinctions: male, female; human, animal; living, dead. One verse might open, "So dig me a grave and dig it so deep . . ." and in the next, "they dug her a grave . . . and maybe by now she's forgotten." A shipwreck lament might embark with the conventional imprecation, "All you who live at home on land, come listen unto me / While I relate of hardships great / All on the raging sea." But by the end of "The Ship Pomona," which Reese found in a ballad sheet and set to new music, we realize that we've been listening to a ghost.

I've been listening to ghosts so long I'm prone to pronounce "Ireland" as "Ohio." Maybe we all slur on the late shift: Reese, Andrews, Bancroft, and Homner: expats from homes that never were. To remind ourselves that we live in the presence of absence, we've forsworn shamrocks, shillelaghs, saints, and *sheela na gigs*, and dubbed our band after a rest stop on Interstate 80 headed west from Youngstown. The place is called Brady's Leap, and if you don't believe me, the inside jacket of our first CD, *The Road to Killeshandra,* mapquests the very parish. Of course, we can't snuff out the rumors: a certain Captain Brady leapt across Ohio to escape Indians; his distant descendant once dunked a basketball against the Cork Blue Demons; a heart-sore Ithacan once biked over the wine-dark sea.

Perhaps we have fed the heart on fantasy, as Yeats laments. The heart's grown brutal from the fare. We know now, living in this America at this time, that brutal can mean coarse as well as violent. I don't boast that art will save us from tyranny, or that we're in danger of succumbing to a surfeit of shamrocks; but the mandate behind *authenticité* always serves a distortion that is oppression's prime requisite.

So, tomorrow night, or the night after that, we'll go back to singing Dafydd and Whitman, Browning and Cathal Buí and Sheridan and Reese. It will be a small gathering. Plenty of seats available.

As for tonight's gig, it'll be fine. We'll hang our green banner, stiffen our spines, and belt out the old tunes, as we do every year. Through the embellishments of Istvan's mandolin, or through the scent of the goatskin drum, or through the intercession of physics, tonight we will harmonize the real and the make-believe. And if the green glare's too much, I'll daydream about strolling down Cayuga Street and Willow Ave, caught up in the fantasy of a return home, feeling as shot through with absence as I did as a child on 194th Street. I'll dwell on the years in Ireland—making friends, tending bar, studying and teaching, and, yes, playing basketball. It did feel like home, but still I would find myself sometimes standing stunned at a crossroads of the here and not.

There really is "a town called Castlemaine," and "a road to sweet Athy," just as the Clancy Brothers sang them. And "One evening of late" I really did "stray out of Bandon / bound for Clonakilty, making my way." Yes, it's true, "At Ballinascarthy some time I delayed," but not to "wet me ould whistle with porter," merely for a petrol stop at a plaza that might as well have been Brady's Leap. As the fuel pulsed through the nozzle, my foot came alive and my tongue found an old melody and I drifted through words and sound that came not from airwaves, nor from the cabinet hi-fi; but from beneath, through knees and hands, into the limbic node, as my head sank to hear them better—the dead, singing—of what is past, and passing, and to come.

EDITED

No one must see this essay while I live. It must stay secret. Bottom drawer. Let them find it buried under key chains, flasks, and porn. The year of reading must not be concurrent with the composition. The time must not be now; I must be late.

While I live, I'm almost out of time. Nothing stays still. I try to slow things down by editing. I pore over the slush pile. I stay inside my skin and outside theirs. I have a page count. But words will not stay still.

I do not remember what I edited out, and what's left in looks somehow vagrant. Unauthorized. I recall everything else. The weather. The butcher paper and the rolltop desk. The slatted windows and the briar smoke and acrid brew. I remember the Royal typewriter and the blue screen and the Moleskine pads. I remember solitaire. E-mail. I remember the calico cat in Berkeley and the geckos in Lubumbashi and the mice in Ballydehob. I remember boredom. I remember doodling. But the sentences crossed out? No. I won't remember deleting these words: the ones some editor won't find when I am dead.

Editing what's there, forgetting what's not, while simultaneously breathing is too much. Nerves demand attention; sight sucks energy and some mornings even the drift of hand to coffee mug is a strain. Not that the alternative illuminates. But at least the dead stay still. For them, whatever is, is. Is that what I want? Without of course being dead.

I was dead, briefly. Nurses shaved my body and wound me in linen and wheeled my gurney into the suburbs of oblivion. The last I heard before they cracked my sternum was the bass G minor of my band's second album's second track, spun from invisible speakers as a rubber glove secured the breathing mask. "Count down," they said.

10   How did you acquire our CD?
9   Do the dead dwell on commercial distribution?
8   This isn't our best number.
7   Will I be hovering near for the next song?
6   . . . [1]

What I learned being dead: No heart hovers near. There is no white light or if there is it doesn't appear until you trespass beyond memory. No familial voices. No hell. Time is not titrated to an instant. There is no instant.

I came to be again, intubated under processed light. There was no more residing in my skin, where strangers had intruded. Time had proceeded for an indeterminate length. Minutes? Years? Maybe the duration of the history of Egypt, which equates to the period between Planck time and the first riff of the third track of *Heart of the Stranger*. I might never catch up.

If you live it, it isn't history. If you remember it, it isn't edited. Yet.

"The Physicist," we call our upright bassist, because he keeps time and grooves electrons. Last night at Irish Bob's[2] as a lime pod moshed in the pit doing "The Unicorn," he stubbed out his Camel and blurted into the mic that in parallel universes everything happens everywhere at once, but no string anywhere plucks the like of this cacaphonical shite.[3]

That's why this essay must stay hidden while I live. I am afraid of being out of time. I am afraid of falling into the pit I edited out. They pluck ghost strings—that horde of would-be words—fingering three dimensions into two. They want everything in. Nothing left out.

Most of all I fear one towering bookwright. He is seven bloodshot feet with a wingspan that cowls the postwar world. He is Achilles's rage. He is Cuchulain's warp spasm.[4] He has brooded a shelf of monographs and sheaves of periodical publications. His penumbra shades a generation. He has composed the definitive poetry on the Holocaust, on the Gulf War, on Native American genocide, on the dying planet, and on 9/11.

I cannot write his name. I'll call him "the Poet."[5]

If I am dead, why can't I write his name?

First, it's hard, while living, to write as if dead, even if I've been, briefly. After all, isn't everyone not living dead briefly? If his mummy were injected with elixir, wouldn't Tut walk again like an Egyptian? Writing keeps time. It bequeaths itself. It implies that somewhere else exists. Bacteria may devour the host and atoms spill into the cosmos, but grasping death while simultaneously writing and editing drains energy. Writing as if dead requires the opposite of faith. It requires that every letter appear in one place all at once.

Second, I fear that some editor will find this document and leak the Poet's identity prematurely. As the Poet's editor—or one of them, since his opus is more than one house can produce—I should promote his work. Perhaps, after my death, the mystery of the unnamed writer will create a buzz and bump sales across the board. But as long as I am extant, his identity must remain concealed.

And last: the Poet is no physicist, but he has undertaken an experiment with cosmic implications. It terrifies. I do not want it uncovered while I live. In a tiny cabin behind his upstate home, in neat longhand, the Poet has composed a comprehensive history of his life. For fifty years, summer and winter, from Nixon to Obama, bachelor to grandfather, punk to laureate, he has scribbled a small mountain of brindled foolscap—estimated at over four million words. He has spent the last year rendering each notebook into typescript. He has contracted a publisher—someone else, not me.[6] The first two volumes have already been released. They are thick as tree trunks, each boasting 800 8 ½ x 13 ½ pages of nine-point type. Three more are in production. I am speechless. Everything is here. Nothing is edited out. "The landscape within," The Poet calls it. "Faith in an inclusive and enabling aesthetic." It requires "a belief in the idea of wholeness." "Everything in the end," the Poet writes, "comes to One."[7] And he means everything. The world, unadulterated and unaltered, is transmogrified from three to two dimensions. The journal is a parallel universe.

Included: meals, gambling, weather, family, teaching, reading, basketball, gossip, clothing, economics, cars, po-biz, uni-biz, dept-biz, sleep, hangovers, nagging injuries, marriage, race relations, household repairs, travel, publishing, aging, music, hospitals, local politics, baseball, TV programs, science, house painting, the inner ear, motorcycles, weddings, doppelgangers, Christmas, coins, the vague hell of the Congo, friends, acquaintances, enemies, plants, wildlife, sounds at night, aliens, semiotics, golf, contracts, religion, existentialism, Freud, Adorno, Mickey Mantle. . . .

Edited:

Last night at Irish Bob's, the Jukebox[8] broke a string to start the third track and I flashbacked to death. The Jukebox didn't miss a beat; he segued into solo and percussion. But I felt a pause. Momentary. Endless. Afterwards, at Lloyd's,[9] I blurted that the second track ended my first life. The band stared. The Physicist's mouth dribbled green foam.

"I never heard 'Heart of the Stranger,'" I confessed.

"Didn't know you listened," said the Jukebox, "from your broke backbeat."

"Did Kinch[10] hear it?" asked the Transylvanian.[11] "He kept real time."

"Ask Schrödinger's cat,"[12] the Physicist said.

In a box upstairs, there is a garage band recording of a third CD no one has heard or seen. We call it "Schrödinger's Cat."

On Lloyd's art deco bar lies the second tome of the Poet's experiment.

"What's this? The Physicist asked.

"Nothing," I said. "Everything."

The Physicist looked at me. The Jukebox looked at the Muse.[13] The Transylvanian looked at the book as if it were a strange beast.

Lately, they've been looking. Maybe they know I'm out of time. It's true the band has no body—just hands and throat—but that doesn't mean that it can't die.

Editors keep secrets. I reveal them now because I'm dead.

10   We don't care about writers, only about books.

9   Writers don't make books. They make stories, poems, plays, and memoirs. We make books.

8   To the editor, the whole work appears in the first line, like DNA.

7   Every fortune cookie we crack open reads, "The Spring Needs River Banks" or "Salt Can't Taste Itself." Or some such.

6   We have a page count. It is the door between universes. It must stay ajar. Not open, not shut. Joyce couldn't see, so he tapped with his ashplant. Homer didn't have the alphabet, so he plucked a lyre. What was Jesus's fingernail scratching in the clay but Luke's page count? It's not what the market will bear. There is a hard count: death.

5   Sometimes we crack open a writer. Then we applaud the writer's name. But the editor inside the writer should get credit too, just like Kinch gets credit. The editor inside Joyce burned Stephen Hero. Virgil's editor singed the Aeneid. Berryman's editor murdered Berryman. Editors count.

You see why the Poet's experiment terrifies. There is no editor. Nothing left out. Every moment is consecutive and equivalent to every other moment. There is no nothing. Death is not brief, it's endless.

Since my first death, I've had a recurring nightmare. Under a dome of processed light, I'm cracked open. Time has passed. I don't know how much. I will always be dead. My atoms will not be released to a distant galaxy but will hover near always.

Not new, this nightmare. It began eons ago with the yearning to hover near forever.

First they tried stone: pyramids, Easter Island, Stonehenge, Machu Picchu. Raw mass raised, unedited.

Then flesh: Osiris, Dionysus, Xipe Totec, Christ. Flay the skin, unsheathe the mystery. But when they cracked open my chest they found none.

Next, iron: Achilles, Alexander, Caesar, Genghis Khan. Burn down the world to brand an earthly name.

But stone, flesh, and iron are crude instruments. The experiment demanded more sophisticated technology. It needed the alphabet. And paper. Reams and reams.

Twice before has the experiment been undertaken by this latest method. The first was Samuel Pepys, an English fop who clocked 2,500 pages of pigeon pie and tallow and piss buckets and smallpox and bumfuckery through a decade of Restoration London. Everything he saw and heard and said and did, he wrote it down. He may have begun innocently: to save the past, just for himself—to slow time's rush. But the task was blinding him. His quandary: lose sight to see forever. He dropped the papers in the bottom drawer.

Months passed. Years. Decades. Life sped up. He couldn't slow things down. One morning Samuel Pepys woke up old. His heart ticked; his sight blurred. It was then that he conceived his plan. The pages must not be diurnal. The world was rife with graphomaniacs scribbling recipes and heartbreaks and encounters and fantasies and illnesses. Unwitnessed, writing was nothing more than building sand castles.

No. The metaphysical compression of three dimensions into two must be reified in print. Print was the way to hover near forever. It was Pepys's own personal pyramid. He contracted one Stephen Cade, Esq., of London, and instructed Mr. Cade to bind the volumes—to preserve, not edit, not abridge.

Now I am petrified. Of 150 London publishers listed from the years of Pepys's first binding, Cade's name does not appear. What became of Stephen Cade, Esq.? Did he go broke? Mad? Did the experiment destroy him? Did he disappear into Pepys's chirography? This is the reason I fear the Poet, even though I'm not the experiment's publisher.

In my nightmare, recording music, or composing poetry, or writing one thing as if it were another—naming my basement bar, for instance, after a movie set— are tiny versions of the Poet's experiment. I fear the band. When the Jukebox riffs, and the Transylvanian picks it up, and the Physicist puts in the beat as if plucking from the air something that already was, are we opening wide a cosmic door, or slamming it shut? In my nightmare, every napkin-note, every haiku, every fan fiction makes me tremble. I am afraid I may no longer be an editor, but an assistant at the Poet's frightful experiment. What will become of me?

10   I will die without knowing I've died
9   I will die but these words will live
8   I will live and no one will know
7   I will live on the brink of dying
6   I will crack open death
5   The Poet will read this.
4   Everything will happen all at once

What *has* become of me? Is there still time? I have been dying for so long—since September 1979, when I first observed the experiment up close. I saw an editor edited. His name was Dr. Robert Hogan, publisher of *The Journal of Irish Literature*, and I was his assistant. Until the experiment swallowed him, Hogan lurked in his basement office in Memorial Hall in the University of Delaware, smoking his pipe, sipping his Jameson, flipping his tiny hands to punctuate jibes. He would have lived out his tenure until fully desiccated were it not for the two million words of the Dublin journal of Joseph Holloway.

A total of 221 volumes. One hundred thousand pages. For a generation they had accreted dust in some mothy hole of the Long Room in the Old Library at Trinity while Kenner, Hone, Ellman, Donohue, Cronin, the Cruiser—every busker in the critical band—hovered near.

Holloway's journal. The journal of Holloway. High-grade, ninety-proof, uncut stream of unconscionable gossip. Forty years Holloway never missed an Abbey Theatre opening. He shadowed Synge and buttonholed O'Casey and worshipped Yeats and ground his teeth at Joyce. When the rabble hurled turnips at *The Playboy*, he scribbled. When the old lady said "No," he jotted. He held a towel when Gogarty swam the Liffey. He snuck backstage to sniff Pegeen Mike's ignominious shift. When Yeats bellowed to the limelights, "Light, at last," it was Holloway yelping back, "But Mr. Yeats the theatre's on fire."

Holloway in the pit, Holloway in the green room. Holloway hanging from the balcony. Ubiquitous. Invisible. The critical band hovered but would not pluck. They were keen-bladed surgical makers of subtraction. They knew better than to let this compostable stack of higher nonsense see the light of print.

Then one fateful sabbatical, Robert Hogan, big-shot Yank professor, materialized with his alligator boots, his steamy specs and his unwillingness to be gainsaid. At the University of Delaware, he may have been an Eng. Dept. creature, but in Dublin, he was a publisher. And Holloway's journal was the tallest peak, the whitest whale, the hardest pancake.

Hogan understood that Holloway had taken measures to upgrade Pepys. First, the Dubliner had scrubbed every entry clean of literary merit. As Hogan wrote, "In style and artistry it is probably one of the worst books ever written."[14]

No accident, the prose. Whereas Pepys wrote with fervor and panache, Holloway took pains so that his chirography would not be mistaken for anything but what it was: a gambit to rob one dimension from the cosmos.

So, Holloway never left his city, limiting the need for description. Unlike Pepys, he made not the least impression on others, facilitating the observation of diverse characters in their native habitat. He did not marry, or philander, or drink, or gamble, or joke. He did not, so to speak, do any actual living at all.

Hogan knew Holloway's behemoth for what it was: the most advanced version yet of the experiment. But he was not afraid. This time, he thought, the editor would triumph. So he unpeeled a wad of Dow Chemical dollars on the unvarnished window snug in Davy Byrnes, poleaxing the Trinity librarians and wrangling the lit. deal of the century. Now Hogan owned the rights to the formula to translate three dimensions into two.

I confess that I was present at the transaction. I spent the following week hunched over the antique Xerox machine in the Old Library until the ultraviolet seared my retina. There were tussles with HDip layabouts and shushes from cassocked monks and several questionable incidents with VAT. But ultimately, we got it home—the Holloway cosmos. And Hogan set about conducting the transfer. He transcribed, collated, justified, commentated. But never did he amend or omit a word.[15]

Hogan was already tiny. The volume of air his form displaced was inconsiderable. But after he returned bearing Holloway's yellowing treasure, he began to shrink. His Stetson brimmed his chin. He swam inside his boots. Only his larynx thrived.

"If literature," he'd rant, flippers churning, "is a puzzle to bring the sublunary"—he launched a spangle of wetness into the air—"to the lip of the eternal," he paused, "then pause is essential to the transaction."

Through impaired nostrils he breathed, then hiccupped twice.

"But, extend artificial utterance—print—indefinitely—the resulting aesthetic buffers truth from beauty and allows unimpeded dimensional transference."

His tongue performed a kind of pirouette.

"Truth is truth, my friend, in whatever species. By means of an exact pairing of scale, literature explodes. Finally, words on the page match perfectly the time to read them. Aristotle's laws have caught up to Einstein's train."[16]

Hogan would go on like this for hours till finally he was no taller than a paragraph, while the reams of Holloway's journal in the windowless office rose ever higher. His final words, seeming to wend up from the billowing journal itself, were "In scope and in content it is one of the most fascinating and valuable documents to emerge from the greatest periods of Irish Letters."[17]

I cannot testify that Robert Hogan's death was actually caused by Holloway's journal. I cannot say even that he went blind. But it is my belief that he was swallowed whole by the landscape within.

What might have saved Hogan?

10   a typewriter with a sticky *e*.

9   a druidic cloud to save the oaks from pulping.

8   boustrophedon.

7   A smallish fence hole and a lion chasing.

6   A sabbatical from sabbaticals.

5   A hundred years of silence.

4   A page count. Call it the Joyce Quotient. Like the NBA salary cap or Obama's emissions quota, a tax should be imposed on anything over 2,122 pages—because really, if ranked qualitatively, has anyone not named Shakespeare written a two thousand one hundred and twenty-third page that's worth a damn?

3   blindness.

But it's useless. Hogan's atoms—as well as my own—have dispersed into pixels.

Cade vanished. Hogan was swallowed. The Poet's publisher? His website is off line and his phone is disconnected.[18]

With every iteration, the experiment becomes more terrifying. The Poet has studied previous attempts and taken measures to ensure the success of his redaction from three-dimensionality to two.

10   He has lived placidly—teaching thirty-five years at the same school and living at the same address, limiting the need to describe different places and objects.

9   He is long married to one wife—whose name is the title of the second volume,[19] obviating the need for coyness, code, or obfuscation.

8   He has not, as Holloway did, abjured life completely. Instead, he has achieved total integration of internal and sensory experience, thus including space for the entirety of his being in the transmogrification. Simply put, he never entertains a thought he wouldn't write.

7   He has anticipated pixels. Print is his control, e-books his variable.

6   He has cultivated a poetic career, thus creating an alibi for the experiment. Who would question a writer writing in a writing cabin?

5   Though his hands are huge, his handwriting is small and linear, thus diminishing the appearance of garrulity.

4   He is skilled at poker, honing his sense of order in randomness.

3   He writes the same number of words at the same time every day, thus ensuring the uniform texture of the interface between worlds.

2   While he transfigures three dimensions into two, I fear that he may be concocting a unified theory. "Everything is One," the Poet says.

1   . . .

Yet, I am still two: living and dead, the reader of what's here and mourner for all that is edited out. I am maker of this essay and its concealer. Band member, and the one who may have broken up the band. How could I be one and be alive?[20]

Maybe Hogan was right. Maybe Pepys and Holloway and the Poet could straighten out truth and beauty. Maybe the band is doing its own experiment, turning sound into a body—and I am the heartbeat, hovering near. "Let me die," the Poet says, "But not die out."

Easy for him to say—he's never died.

It occurs to me that leaving this essay in the bottom drawer may not be the best way to ensure that it is found after my death. Movers will come, or the Salvation Army, or a wrecking ball. There will be no literary executor. No archive. Perhaps best to place it in some university press book, where I can be sure it won't be read now, but perhaps—just perhaps—it may be found one day on some doctor's waiting room table or some 5&10 sale or even in the basement of the English Department of the University of Delaware.

I am down to one. I am going where no word is any worse than any other. [21]

Notes

1. The band referred to is most probably Brady's Leap, a New-Celtic group from Youngstown, Ohio, in which Brady played bodhrán. Their second CD was *Heart of the Stranger* (Rosewood Studios, 2004). The third track is the title song, based on Walt Whitman's Civil War diary. The line referenced is "Little he knew, poor death-stricken boy, / the heart of the stranger of that hovered near."
2. Irish Bob's is a bar on Youngstown's South Side. Along with other internal evidence, the reference to this gig places the time of the essay at March 18, 2015.
3. Dr. James Andrews, Distinguished Professor of Physics, Youngstown State University, played in Brady's Leap from 2001–2016. The anecdote is clearly apocryphal since Dr. Andrews doesn't speak on stage, nor does he smoke.
4. "The first warp-spasm seized Cúchulainn, and made him into a monstrous thing, hideous and shapeless, unheard of. His shanks and his joints, every knuckle and angle and organ from head to foot, shook like a tree in the flood or a reed in the stream. His body made a furious twist inside his skin, so that his feet and shins switched to the rear and his heels and calves switched to the front. . . . On his head the temple-sinews stretched to the nape of his neck, each mighty, immense, measureless knob as big as the head of a month-old child . . . he sucked one eye so deep into his head that a wild crane couldn't probe it onto his cheek out of the depths of his skull; the other eye fell out along his cheek. His mouth weirdly distorted: his cheek peeled back from his jaws until the gullet appeared, his lungs and his liver flapped in his mouth and throat, his lower jaw struck the upper a lion-killing

blow, and fiery flakes large as a ram's fleece reached his mouth from his throat. . . .
The hair of his head twisted like the tangle of a red thorn bush stuck in a gap;
if a royal apple tree with all its kingly fruit were shaken above him, scarce an
apple would reach the ground but each would be spiked on a bristle of his hair
as it stood up on his scalp with rage" (trans. Thomas Kinsella, *The Tain*, Oxford
University Press, 1973).

5. William Heyen

6. H_NGM_N Books

7. William Heyen, *Hannelore* (H_NGM_N Books, 2015), 7.

8. Dr. Steven Reese, English Professor at Youngstown State University. All songs
on *Heart of the Stranger* (Rosewood Studios, 2004), as well as eight tracks on
Brady's Leap's debut CD, *The Road to Killeshandra* (Rosewood, 2002), were composed and arranged by Dr. Reese, who led the band and its predecessor, Shillelagh
Law, from 1991–2016.

9. A prohibition-style, art deco wet bar in the basement of a ramshackle cottage on
the Northside of Youngstown, where Brady lived from 2008–2016. The name de-
rives from the ghostly bartender in *The Shining*.

10. Timothy Hunter, M.D. performed triple bypass surgery on the author on October
11, 2010. In *Ulysses*, "Kinch" (the knife blade) is Buck Mulligan's cognomen for Stephen Dedalus.

11. Istvan Homner, accomplished mandolin player and devotee of the gold standard
and predestination, produced both Brady's Leap CDs at Rosewood Studios, located
in his refurbished basement in New Castle, PA.

12. "A thought experiment, sometimes described as a paradox, devised by Austrian
physicist Erwin Schrödinger in 1935. It illustrates what he saw as the problem
of the Copenhagen interpretation of quantum mechanics applied to everyday
objects. The scenario presents a cat that may be simultaneously both alive and
dead, a state known as a quantum superposition, as a result of being linked to a
random subatomic event that may or may not occur. The thought experiment is
also often featured in theoretical discussions of the interpretations of quantum
mechanics" (Wikipedia).

13. Kelly Bancroft, lead singer of Brady's Leap. Bancroft is married to Steve Reese,
"The Jukebox."

14. Robert Hogan, ed., *Joseph Holloway's Abbey Theatre* (Carbondale: Southern Illinois
University Press, 1967), 7.

15. Hogan did in fact edit Holloway's Journal and cut it considerably. The tale of meeting an unnamed librarian at Davy Byrnes's pub seems apocryphal. Dow Chemical did not endow the liberal arts at the University of Delaware in 1979. They did,
however, finance university experiments with napalm.

16. There is no source for these quotes, though they do sound like that odd little elf,
Hogan. The oblique and uninformed dropping of Einstein's name probably references his metaphor of a train moving at near light speed.

17. Cribbed directly from Hogan's introduction to *Joseph Holloway's Abbey Theatre*, p. 8.
18. Nate Pritts founded H_NGM_N Books. The website is rudimentary, but live.
19. *Hannelore.*
20. Theories abound regarding the breakup of Brady's Leap. Some claim that Brady's arhythmical bodhrán finally drove Reese and Andrews mad; others point to the nonappearance of Schrödinger's Cat as causal or symptomatic of dysfunction. But as former band member William Greenway notes, "Everything has a lifespan. Sound dies."
21. On March 18, 2016, one year after the band's last performance at Irish Bob's, Philip Brady disappeared from his position as Distinguished Professor of English at Youngstown State University. He simply did not show up for a Thursday evening graduate class in literary editing. Attempts to contact him at his office have been unsuccessful. Rumors swirl. A tall, bald, motley-clad Caucasian has been seen wandering the Queens Botanical Garden. Other reports place him in Ballydehob, West Cork, and there have been sightings in Bukavu and Brigadoon. Twelve cartons of paper covered in indecipherable handwriting, thought to be committed in boustrophedon, an arcane code without spaces or left–right orientation, have been unearthed behind Lloyd's bar. Some scholars believe this trove contains all the words Brady edited out. Others think that this is his own attempt at the experiment, conducted over twenty-five years, and that even now he searches for a publisher. The most popular belief is that he is dead. The editor of the imprint under which this essay appears is of this opinion, and therefore finds it appropriate to publish posthumously. The means whereby this essay was acquired must remain confidential. I can say only that it would make a ripping good story, and perhaps, after my death, it can be told.

MY PHANTOM NOVELIST

My imaginary friend is a brilliant novelist. Not in the "He has said so himself" way. Everyone says so.

"Brilliant," they buzz around my ears, along with all the usual treacle— "stunning," "breathtaking"—and of course that sweetest gumdrop, "poetic."

Well, not really everyone. My imaginary friend's brilliance is a secret shared by a small club of luminaries, including an esteemed biographer, a laureled poet, a hedge funder, my matrilineal namesake famous writer, a former teammate of Pelé, and the ghost of John Gardner. Outside this circle, my figment is internationally unknown. No beach reader, fic-fan, tweeter, or celebrity stalker has heard his name.

In fact, only now am I ready to christen my imaginary friend, though three decades have passed since the moonlit night when he first appeared. In Gorse tweed and fedora, sporting a Harley moustache you could weaponize, he buzzed the doorbell and shouldered in, sloshing a martini big as a lampshade. Without preface, he flopped on the couch and set right into cantillating "The Death of Cuchulain," and he hasn't paused longer than two gulps ever since. But, through all the schemes, heart-to-hearts, and escapades, I never settled on a name.

It's tricky, naming phantoms. After all, everyone has imaginary friends, and some of us script dialogue and fabricate life stories, and endow motive and agency, but baptism may be a bridge too loony.

Still, I have made a few attempts.

"Dim," I muttered as he snored in a beach tent. But at that moment, a wave crashed over the canvas, and Dim never stuck. It got me started though.

"Mr. Nearweather?" I tapped his sleeve in an opium den.

"No," he replied. "Too Dickensian."

"Count Forthenonce?" I queried in a castle.

"It is true that I am not."

"Indeterminator!" I yelped as we raced sirens on the freeway.

"Too Arnold," he bawled into the wind.

But I've got it now. In memory of that first moonlit night, I'll call him Mooney. While Mooney is, unfortunately, also the name of a real-world novelist who is also coincidentally a friend, that can't be helped. Mooney it is. And anyway, this sleight of hand is the kind of thing novelists might like.

A part of me would like to confer on Mooney fame and success. At sixty-two (we have the same birth date) I'd have him hale and spry. He's a former linebacker and marathoner. His consumption of spirits is tamped to unheroic levels by his "Lass," and his children—a boy and a girl—are well fledged. The students at his bucolic college revere him; he makes pilgrimages to his aged mother and his Jesuit mentor.

Like Joyce, he has committed three novels. His debut, *The Well at the End of the World*, is a literary thriller set in an upstate burg where Dutch Potter, a bus driver and D-Day veteran, is slowly losing his mind with grief for his son Jom, MIA in Vietnam. Finally, after endless letters and phone calls to Washington, Dutch dons his WWII uniform, pockets a souvenir grenade, and swerves off route, hijacking his busload of passengers over state lines, where he slams into a tree and bolts the door, provoking a federal hostage crisis. Dutch has three demands: 1. Bring back my son. 2. Bring back my son. And you get #3. At 690 pages, *The Well at the End of the World* is a beast; its speedster plot careens through the claptrap lives of straphangers, and the rustification of their town, and the timeless suffering which draws us to the well at the world's end.

Of praise, I wish an elegant sufficiency. Nothing louche. No crudité or Oprah. Maybe a few spots on local NPR. Some robust bookstore signings. An advance big enough to fix the car. I want a gunslinger agent and a white-shoes editor; I want a publisher who yields on cover design, and bloodhound copyeditors who find, for instance, that the Rambo flick on page 310 actually debuted a year later. I want a star from *Publishers Weekly* and minimal snark from *Kirkus*. I want warm ovations and rich silence and permission to daydream that the sexy eyes of the park-bench reader Mooney jogs past are a tad moist. I want the Lass to look up adoringly and say, "I can't believe *you* wrote this."

And of course it's not all about the reception. There's the semigloss jacket; the picnic grin on the French flap; the cream pages with their justified margins; the sentences in their noble Garamond. At the Strand, the gaze of my imaginary friend bathes in his own chirography, each phrase pitched above an almost audible thrum. Closing his tome, he declines to mount the ladder to reshelve between Moon and Moorcock. Instead he strides to the atrium and places the remaindered copy, bookmark high, on the new releases table.

All this I want for *The Well at the End of the World.*

But in my seventh decade, it is not meet to dwell in fantasy. *The Well at the End of the World* is a long book—big as a double-decker—by an unknown writer who has not taken the precaution of placing stories in *The New Yorker.* Such offerings do not cross the desks of hustling agents and urbane editors and clammy reviewers. And Mooney, for all his dash, has debts and kids and a tenure committee and a sensitive soul. I fear for him. I fear the well will be poisoned. I fear that pretend friends from the real world will interrogate Mooney until he slashes, repackages, and perhaps even retitles. I am afraid that Universe City will get its mitts on Mooney.

Yet, without at least a soupçon of success, how can he go on? Would sheltering *The Well* dim Mooney's light?

Other voices clamor to intrude. Pretend friends point out that *The Well at the End of the World* lacks ISBN or PCIP or list price or marketing or Amazon page or swag. Sales are in single digits. Actually, 0. *The Well at the End of the World,* pretend friends sneer, does not technically exist. It is merely a redaction of other texts. Googling yields four such knock-offs.

William Morris's *The Well at the World's End* (1896), charts a mystical journey—not unlike Dutch Potter's—to a destination where time and identity disappear. A. J. Mackinnon's *The Well at the World's End* (Black Inc., 2010) follows the author's off-road adventures from Australia to a legendary Scottish village; while *The Well at the End of the World* by Robert D. San Souci and illustrated by Rebecca Walsh (Chronicle Books, 2013) delineates, for readers on Fountas & Pinnell level P-7, the exploits of Princess Rosamond, whose no-nonsense management of her father's kingdom calls to mind Dutch's bearish handling of his passengers.

The most striking parallel is a novel entitled *Father of the Man* (Pantheon, 2002) which involves a bus driver named Dutch Potter, who, like Dutch Potter, crashes into an out-of-state tree to force the government to produce his son, also named Jom. Further coincidences must be acknowledged. The author of *Father of the Man* is the real-world Mooney, who as I stipulated is a close friend and cofounder of Etruscan Press. Real World Mooney also shares some strands of biography with Imaginary Mooney, including a family, teaching career, and a perilous thirst.

However, two significant differences distinguish I. M. (Imaginary) Mooney's *The Well at the End of the World* from R. W. (Real World) Mooney's novel. First, *Father of the Man* lacks the heft of *The Well at the End of the World*. It does not meander through myriad lives—card-sharp Whitey and shift-nurse Bess and teen-mom Cardia and blind Jehosaphat, whose entangled calamities give *The*

Well at the End of the World the feel of an epic unearthed from some prehistoric bus station. Keenly novelistic, *Father of the Man* employs sharp, imagistic prose to sketch an arc from Dutch's WWII D-Day—concurrent with the birth of his son—to his personal D-Day confrontation with the feds.

The second difference is, I believe, more telling. As part of his exhaustive research, R. W. interviewed FBI agents to see how they would resolve a real-world standoff. The G-Men were accommodating. After all, what real-world character doesn't want to be fictionalized? The suits leaned forward and took notes as R. W. laid out the scene.

In the summer forest, no sniper can get a clear shot. The suspect grips an unpinned live grenade. He has studied FBI tactics and protocol. He knows to refuse proffered provisions. He knows not to brook promises or delay; he knows, deep in his heart, the futility of his demand. He is prepared to die, and perhaps also to kill.

Then, a plot twist. Jom's childhood friend arrives. Meehan resembles Jom and is intimately familiar with his life's story. Child of a broken home, Meehan has always envied the close-knit Potter clan. He yearns to be Jom. Dutch is a surrogate father.

Meehan, proposed R. W., could pose as Jom. Jom has been missing for many years and Dutch is desperate to believe. Meehan as Jom can lure Dutch from the bus, assuring the grief-crazed father that his son has come home. If probed with intimate questions, Meehan can answer convincingly.

The agents conferred. R. W. sweated.

Finally, they returned a verdict. "Negative."

Civilians, they disclosed, were never permitted within operational zones. Instead, they recommended an alternative plan: an undercover agent, disguised as Jom and wired for two-way transmission, will cross the perimeter. If questioned, the agent can receive Meehan's responses through his earpiece. The agent will apprehend the suspect and secure the hostages. Meehan will remain at all times in the command center.

Thus, in *Father of the Man*, it came to be.

Imaginary Mooney's research was inhibited by his insubstantial nature. No agent, organization, website, entity, or citizen of the real world was consulted during the long slow years of composition. In a moonlit mind, *The Well at the End of the World* deepened until it filled the imaginary world. Yes, the protagonist was Dutch, but he was also Odysseus, questing out of state to save his son. Jom was MIA in Vietnam, but also Telemachus in Ithaca.

But Imaginary Mooney has no purchase on the real world. For him, there can be no homecoming. Telemachus can never embrace his father. *The Well at the End of the World* renders the reality inside imagination, the place from which no one returns. Thus Meehan—Jom's phantom sign—takes Jom's place and receives the benediction. The touch of Dutch's hand consecrates Meehan as Jom and both as Telemachus. In moonlight, Mooney reflects Mooney. This consubstantiation—more than the high lyricism and Melvillian girth and violation of FBI protocol—marks the place where *The Well at the End of the World* breaks with all other versions, and with the genre of fiction itself.

What is a novel? This is not a question for a dinner party or a ballgame or a lover's ear. In times of joy and communion, it's poetry we invoke.

"Invites a certain kind of attention . . . takes the top of your head off . . . begins with a lump in the throat . . . a tongue swirl on numinal labia . . . a Michael Jordan fadeaway."

Poems, it appears, do not require bodies, only phantom signs: heed, shock, love, lust, or grace. Novels must encompass the real world. Pages must turn. Gears grind. Characters deploy. Sentences wend. Minds and landscapes must be mapped and bound in a dynamic facsimile of everything witnessed or imagined.

Deprived of time and light, novels are null. Before e-books, I would have said that a novel must be a thing, but even pixels require the idea of thingness. Yes, there is rhythm and image and nodes of silence; but these take place within the frame of thingness. Do novels unbound even exist? Was *Ulysses* non-existent before Darantiere, the printer? The *Iliad* before Homer? How many phantom novels stalk the world?

To be, a novel must be read. It must aggregate appreciable numbers. If a novel falls in the forest and no one hears, it is a poem.

Yet, if for no other reason than my need to advance to Mooney's next novel, I close my eyes and swear that *The Well at the End of the World* exists. If I must spend my last penny of faith to back its thingness, so be it. Imaginary production is on-going. Imaginary marketing churns. Imaginary reception proliferates with a throng of perfect readers—imaginary me's—who had not realized, before we read *The Well*, that nothing could encompass all.

I open my eyes. Presto. Mooney moves forward—and how! In weight and ambition, Mooney's next enterprise dwarfs *The Well*.

Most importantly, *Going Out Foreign* indubitably exists.

"*Across the mad scribbling of the sea*, McMullen thought, agitated, bewildered, *a rough draft of November*--that was it--and, widening his stance against the ferry's yaw, he wrote this thought in the notepad he kept in the back right pocket of his dungarees, adding *Samhain 1978, 10:42 a.m.*, scribbling madly himself, as I am now, when the man in the wheelchair--who had been spying him since they boarded at Stranraer--motored his contraption across the foredeck, playing the yaw like a difficult putt, crooking his head from the jittering helix of his body as if crooning the same Clancy Brothers song playing all morning in McMullen's head. The wheel grazed McMullen's ankle as he parked at the railing, jerked his head skyward and--spittle flying like sea spray--asked if he, McMullen, would be his friend."

Drenched in mad scribbling of unsolicited submissions and at the same time bewildering an agitation of students and also yawing through our own rough drafts, publishers who also teach and write widen our first glance to encompass the whole text. One strand must reveal the jittering helix, lest we drown beneath typhoons of e-docs, like Mooney in a pup tent. One glance. One paragraph, from which we glean the whole book. Does it tingle the scalp? Swell throat and labia? Shoot the moon?

In this microcosm, I spy the entire *Going Out Foreign,* novel-cum-memoir-cum-postmodern text, as if Imaginary Mooney had taken one Olympian breath and recited, between Yeats bits, all 460 typed pages.

In Mooney's time past—*"1978, 10:42 a.m."*—I hear McMullen's pilgrimage to escape family dysfunction to find his true self, for which purpose he keeps a notebook, purloined by his handicapped doppelganger. I intuit the gallop around Ireland: like Mad Sweeney hopping treetops, McMullen leaps from the IRA to Yeats's grave into the arms of a mythic sexpot from the Sidhe.

In time present—"as I am now" I sniff his admission of the frangibility of texts—the novelist as scribbler—and his return home, his withering into truth as he meets and dates and marries the Lass, and then closes the all-encompassing codex with a waft of Gardner's pipe smoke.

In the "crooning . . . in McMullen's head," I sense the yearning to evoke the thingness of the novel—time ticking within timelessness that is the spittle sea spray of Clancy tunes and druidic Halloween—the nothing without which novels are mere objects. And in the double hyphens for dashes I detect the orthographic authenticity: this text has been touched by Mooney's luddite hands.

Then, a twist. Imagine me on a bar stool next to Imaginary Mooney in full swing, deep into his sea spray spittle recitation.

He stops. He jerks his head skyward. "What, do you think, pal, is the name McMullen takes to keep his true identity from his sidekick?"

"What?" says I, a bit dizzy.

"I'll tell," says Mooney, "But first tell me. Do you think *Going Out Foreign* is the real thing?"

"I do," I say. "There's not only the indubitable text and the magical turns and time-defying plot and morphing characters and indelible landscapes and lyric prose and orthographic signature."

"True for you," says Mooney.

"Other persons," I attest, "have endorsed."

From the back right pocket of my dungarees I draw the blurbs.

> "*Going Out Foreign* is one of those great rattle bags of a novel, with rhythm, style, pacing, humor, empathy, bravery, and depth."
>
> —Matrilineal Namesake Famous Writer

> "The characters come alive instantly, to Mooney's immense credit. As does Ireland, a character in itself."
>
> —Esteemed Biographer

> "Mooney is a supremely talented writer, and in Daniel McMullen, he has constructed a strong protagonist whom you sympathize with as he travels throughout Ireland struggling to come to an understanding of his place in the world. I also thought he did a nice job of depicting the harsh realities of the region and the intricacies of the landscape, as well as providing a slew of colorful characters that Daniel encounters in his travels."
>
> —The Ghost of John Gardner

> "*GOF* rocks, man."
>
> —Rock Star

> "*Going Out Foreign* is the next huge bear."
>
> —Hedge Funder

> "Que palhaçada . . . Gol!"
>
> —Former Teammate of Pelé

"So," says Mooney, as I pocket the scroll, "the name McMullen puts on himself is the same as the one on the title page, same as punched into Library of Congress, same as my international passport, the same as the ould one in 'The Boarding House': 'Mooney.'"

"Oh," I say, and faint.

When I come to, I am sick with the need to address real-world readers of this essay, who may object that I christened Mooney on page 1, but cite the soubriquet here as if composed—in any sublunary timeline—before this essay began.

What, real-world readers ask, is an essay?

If a novel requires thingness, and poems employ signs, an essay needs an author. In Universe City, the author hides behind the curtain of We. Stripped to my boxers, I pretend to be I. The more candid and entertaining my *I*, the more engaged your *you*.

But who can be fully candid among strangers?

Only the mortally sinless can be *I*. No one would read an essay by an I the child molester, I rapist, I the tobacco executive or I provost: accounts from these sources must be fictionalized, as in novels like *The Collector* or *Lolita* or *American Psycho* or *A Clockwork Orange* (even novelists can't dig provosts). If these were nonfiction, we'd call the cops. But if essays are written only by the mortally sinless, then we miss the experience of the majority of the population, who are not.

Part of me wants this snaggled timeline to stand for essayists who are gleefully sinful, an underrepresented demographic. Yet in my seventh decade, I am not content with one explanation for any phenomenon.

Even mortally sinful essayists must base their work on poetic or novelistic principles. As essays present timeless ideas, they are poetic. As they are constructed of sentences and imply narrative, they are novelistic. If the clock in the novel ticks constantly, and poetic clocks hum in cloud–cuckoo land, in essays clocks lag and lurch, and even the real-world reader consents to blink.

I blink. Then I stare. On-screen appears essay and poem and novel and Facebook and e-mail and fake news and scores. It is real. It is pixels. No wonder contemporary novels and poems and essays crossbreed.

For instance, imagine me trolling Kardashian when the screen pops an e-mail from R. W. He is having a hard time with his second novel, the story of a young American going to Ireland to find his roots. His protagonist, named McMullen, wanders Ireland in search of self and also in pursuit of a notebook, pickpocketed by a dude in a motorized wheelchair. *Going Out Foreign*, it's called. The trick is that McMullen takes on the alias Mooney. Get it?

I stare at the screen. The screen stares back.

It is perhaps almost possible to believe that two novels featuring a bus driver named Dutch Potter and recounting a federal hostage scene, however differently resolved, might exist independently. But it is absolutely inconceivable that two novelists, both named Mooney, would follow that coincidence with another novel featuring identical titles and parallel plots, both using Mooney as a false name for a fictional character.

Are R. W. and I. M. colluding behind my back? It wouldn't be impossible, as

I have dozed many an afternoon on R. W.'s porch. Easy for I. M. to slip out and confab with R. W. Worse, both I. M. and R. W. use the same device: pretending to be Mooney. But which one—I. M. or R. W.? Is R. W. trying to become I. M. just as I. M. sneaks off with R. W.?

Of course, Imaginary Mooney is cleverer than I am. What would be the point of having an imaginary friend who isn't? Is he cramped in my brain's accommodations? Does he long for more elaborate passages? For congress with a real-world novelist? Does he spelunk in R. W.'s keener ear? And what about R. W.? Will he filch my figment to break the logjam of his novel's draft?

I forgive them both. I cling to one shred. In significant ways, I. M.'s *Going Out Foreign* differs from R. W.'s *Going Out Foreign*.

In I. M.'s book, phantom signs are real. McMullen, Mooney, the Lass, Gardner's Ghost, the sex kitten from the Sidhe, the IRA hit men, Yeats patrolling his grave, and romantic Ireland alive and dead yaw toward us on a current of rhythmic utterance. I. M.'s *Going Out Foreign* shows that while novels are things, they are not mere things or even a mirror of things; but rather, as Mooney mutters, "mirror on mirror mirrored."

R. W.'s *Going Out Foreign* must contend with the real world. Yes, he has tenure, and the kids are grown, but his soul is still vulnerable to pretend friends counseling homogeneity, realism, and tact.

"Doesn't need . . ." they buzz. "Would be stronger . . ." they chorus.

"Peel . . . cut . . . sections . . . tighten more intimate . . . people may not see . . . conceptual critique . . . too many at once . . . unessential . . . cleaner . . . accountable . . . the whole thing can go."

While I. M. guzzles moonshine and channels Yeats, R. W. revises. His Mooney takes on the cognomen Tavish. Gardner is whited out. The Lass is backgrounded. Even the sea creature has to apply for a visa.

Agents and editors close in.

"Not convinced . . . quite well written . . . wasn't drawn. . . . unappealing . . . Lou flat . . . brief attempts to give life . . . half-hearted . . . evocation . . . beautiful, but . . . shame that . . . lyrical ear . . . thought it would be huge . . . smaller and smaller. . . . promising, I'm afraid. . . . I fear . . . as I would need to be . . . impressive, never hooked . . . utmost care . . . have to be enthralled. . . . Given reservations, must allow . . .

And there it stands, stranded. The real-world *Going Out Foreign* is as far from thingness as Imaginary Mooney.

Last comes *Swamproot*. I don't know who started it or when, but it features two characters, one real world and one imaginary, neither named Mooney. They communicate by notebook from a distant past, which the real world still revises. They flow together like the river from which words spring, though who knows when or where or if they will ever end.

"The river Kraker is on his way to die in starts out of the glacier-gouged lake into a confusion of circumstances beginning with its name: *Susquehanna* ("long-reach river?" "long crooked river?" "place of the straight river?" "mud river?") gathering itself through bogs and swampy lakes across the highlands of upstate New York, gliding over sandstone and shale, moraines and terraces, plateaus of orderly rock into canoe-shaped valleys bosomed in Pennsylvanian hills before turning back north and west along New York's southern tier through Binghamton, a burg built on cigars and shoes and a snake oil called Swamp Root where it takes on the southering Chenango, another native word for another river, Oneidan, meaning "bull-thistle," just that, toward which, a quarter mile north, he staggers full stride, blood slathered over his face and neck and the overcoat he's wearing despite the heat. Boarded buildings echo sirens saying he's done for, though what's happened feels only as real as the fluttering of pixels on a screen."

I do not know if the pixels flutter into four novels or one. All are out of print, though once on a high shelf in a bookish bar, I glimpsed the orange bus–cover spine of *Father of the Man* and I peeled Imaginary Mooney from his pint to show him the thing his namesake had wrought.

We paged. We read soundlessly. We were all three together.

I do not know where the novel ends. Maybe all novels yaw through swamps out foreign to the well at the world's end to meet the father of the man. Mired in primal mud, they are not mere things. They are here. They are going. They flow through everyone imagined. They flow toward everyone and everything that's not.

LINE & SENTENCE

Sometimes sentences and lines • need to be the same.
—H. L. Hix

A few years ago, at the age of fifty-two, I married for the first time. In the old days, in the old country, this wouldn't have been strange: a bachelor might brood for decades. But in this century, marrying at my age is less likely than being struck by lightning. Which, I suppose, is the same thing.

Not diffidence, nor fastidiousness, nor sloth kept me single. You see, I am a changeling. Neither male nor female, we changelings drift beyond the magnetic pull of the primary sexes, where we undergo a gestation almost as long and excruciating as a novelist.

Not that I am a novelist, or even a distant cousin. But they too claim a separate sex. Poised above their fragile creations, novelists cannot afford gendered bodies; instead, they aspire to evanesce, like Joyce's self-manicuring god. But divinity's a bit much, I think, even for Joyce. Changelings are hardly deities. We're just not completely here.

This musing about sex has been brought on by a new book, *The Widening*, by the poet Carol Moldaw. A novel, she calls it, and I'll take her at her word. Written in lightning-quick vignettes from an interior third-person point of view, *The Widening* follows an unnamed female protagonist through a painful adolescence. From the memorable first sentence, "At the crucial moment she said yes," through 148 pages of self-scrutiny, *The Widening* reveals the power and vulnerability of new womanhood in the crucible of the sexual revolution. To say this book is about sex is true, and also completely wrong—not because it isn't. But saying a book is about sex implies a prurience, which is a brand of purity achieved when bodies are pressed together and portrayed, so that boundaries are made clear. This is the mission, I'm informed, of the pornographer. Intent on objectivity, the pornographer—or perhaps, more gently, the eroticist—steps behind a lens, opening a space from which the intimacies of the gendered can be framed.

Of course, to us changelings, all novels revel in smut. Vanilla, kinky, gay, trans—no matter. They're all subtitled; "Skin, Bound"; their theme: Skin Bound Seeks Release. The urge's thwarting twists into a plot. Are novels inherently lurid? We of the tertiary gender nod our heads.

And in this light, I wonder if Carol Moldaw's lapidary offering is a novel at all. Remarkably ascetic when it comes to flesh, she never steps behind a verbal camera to register perspective. Each chapter—and given that the longest is three hundred words, "chapter" seems a big-shouldered label—distills a moment; each is discrete, their cumulative power deriving from the pattern of drift, like motes across a field of vision. Against the edifice of the novel, these light-spots dance elusively, never quite coalescing into anything as conventional as a plot. Maybe *The Widening* isn't a "Skin-Bound" production after all.

Yet, the illusion of narrative conjured by these chapters flows like a field of energy over the sole character's outline. Her age is sixteen to eighteen. There are hip-huggers, a drab brown dress. A ring is slammed over her knuckle, then chained under her blouse. There are bedrooms; backpacks; dorms; a trip through Spain; a journal violated; cigarillos; moderate weight gain; nipples bitten and licked; semen swallowed; and a nose, unbobbed. We know these things in the immediacy in which they are received. And while the character is sole in the sense that hers is the only mind we enter, other voices purport to define her: rich parents, shrinks, and a murder of boys, all acting as stimulants, irritants, agents of action or occasions of reflection. They engorge; they flay. But none attains dimension or characterhood. Ultimately, these forces crystallize into two adjectives that ring like a pair of slaps—"privileged" and "promiscuous."

As a teen, I was not promiscuous. We changelings aren't neuter, though. Inside our hulls, desire oscillates so fiercely we can fritz out like a TV screen. And in that cone we hive. Sight, we do not miss. Bright tinctures swirl; shapes loom and dissolve, prescient beyond the solar world. Nor do we lack touch, self-caressed. For music—there's tinnitus. What we lust after is simply to be desired. For us, every gendered body is privileged. The prime gendered tend to take their flesh for granted, assuming it is universally bestowed. We know better. Occasionally, desire drives a changeling to elbow the glass hatch, crack it open, and gain weak purchase among the binary. The rest stay spooned at the birth portal. Either way, I'm not sure what is forged out of such incubation. But now that I'm married, I feel invited to wonder.

Maybe I was born a changeling. I was a blue baby, whisked from the womb and sequestered in a glass tube to be transfused. Two weeks I lay in a hospital chrysalis, quilled with IV's, while fluids of diverse flavors coursed through veins, pulsing to cure my urge to swim back. Even today, when I set my sleep machine to "surf," I feel the pull of exsanguination.

Or perhaps my nature waxed more slowly. It was no widening, my childhood: growth was relentless, but only in one direction. I spindled upward but gained no more mass than a Slinky. Fearing the skyward sprawl, I folded my limbs and tried to seed. But soon my toes sprang beyond my lips, and I had to wave them goodbye forever. Yearning to scuttle home through the beaker's neck, I hummed, scrawled, chanted, mewed. At the school bus stop, I gripped my book bag's handle and spun like an umbrella. Assigned to the back row, I crafted my fingers into boats and canoes, undulating to the distant drone of nuns. Then I scurried home to spell the dark, devout as an Aztec, by rocking on hands and knees in front of the cabinet hi-fi. Back and forth, haunches to palms, I rocked.

And rocked. Every plunge backward was met by the thud of spongy flesh on bone, spurring the next thrust forward.

Rocking, I discovered lines. Dripping with afterbirth, these tensile entities self-conceived, foamed a few beats, and welcomed their own ebb. Soon, I began to see them everywhere: on cereal boxes and store windows, on cans and baseball bats and T-shirts—even inscribed in the exhausts of acrobatic airplanes. They weren't sentences diagrammed by nuns or spewed by newsmen. Lines might grace paper, but pages didn't shape them. Each had its own axis. Each bar modulated the last and next.

Carol Moldaw did not subtitle *The Widening* "A Prose Poem." A poet of considerable powers, she may have been tempted. The chapters display the texture and poise of stanzas. The voice is liquid, untethered to persona, gliding through amniotic air like my fingers' seacraft. Moldaw dives into sensation, then surfaces to map new constellations. But the paradox of the prose poem—this, she eschews. "If they're lines, why string them out?" I imagine her demanding.

What are prose poems, anyway? Can they rock? Or do their sentences force them to crawl? Have they tumbled from meter into matter? Or do they entwine, partaking of both? Maybe genres are not determined by conventions any more than arms are defined by sleeves. Is *Walden* a prose poem? *Remembrance of Things Past?*

One morning, I could no longer rock. As I sank to my heels, pain shot through my legs. Adolescence, it seemed, had been unraveling my bones until femur unlatched tibia. Osgood-Schlatter disease, they diagnosed, snuffing out my final attempt to retard maturity. By eighth grade, I had sprouted to mannish height, but was as cranky as an arthritic squeezebox. And I started to read novels.

Novelists. Changelings they may be, but they don't crouch at the nub. Their craving glues them to the glistening pane, even if all they see is glare. Our tribe is suspicious, but we're grateful too. We need novels. How else can we learn the manners of the binary? With their compound eyes, novelists observe the fetid, and we study their findings the way a Texan tourist might swat for a Japanese tea ceremony. We've seen all the stunts: epistle, maguffin, yarn, frame—and realisms minimal, maximal and magical. So *The Widening*'s warped contours don't baffle. Let there be longer ellipses. Let the voice be enigmatic as a Pharaoh. Let chapters suffer more radical truncation. Let *The Widening* be engulfed. That is the way of the novel, isn't it? To engulf other forms? So says Citizen Bakhtin. Let there be paragraphs, chapters, sections, sequels. Stamp them like malls. Package them as smartly as Burger King dispatches the rain forest. As for the voice, that's an old dodge, "the unreliable narrator." If the scenes are fragmented and the secondary characters flat, isn't that the point? It's Skin Bound in the sublunary. The author? Poof! I can almost taste a whiff of irony in the cobalt smoke.

But wait. The girl in *The Widening* seldom speaks. The sparse dialogue is italicized, embedded in description. The girl is not the narrator. So whose voice are we listening to? And if *The Widening* isn't a novel or a prose poem, what could it be? If I had knees, I might rock the answers loose.

Carol Moldaw could have dubbed *The Widening* a memoir. That's a popular choice these days. I don't have the dope on her personal life, and can't say if the events chronicled are sufficiently autobiographical to pass the Oprah test. Clues can be sleuthed from the paperback: bio, PCIP, blurbs, promo pic. The author falls within the target age group, the correct gender. She attended Harvard, the locale of part of the novel; she grew up in California, the protagonist's home. And the young girl is a budding poet, as the author is a mature one. Something, perhaps, to go on. But not enough.

Maybe it's the memoir, not the novel, that engulfs. Maybe we see through the façade of fiction the way a shrink sees through the patient who says, "I have this friend with a problem." Chinua Achebe thought so. He raged against *Heart of Darkness*, claiming that Marlow was nothing more than Conrad's mouthpiece. What got under Achebe's skin, I think, is the notion that a world—or in this case, Africa—could be constructed from outside, and that a novelist could evade the consequences of living in his fabrication. Achebe knew those consequences all too well: Africa shriveled to the lobe of a Euro-brain. Rapping on the window safeguarding Conrad from his "unreliable narrator," Achebe bellowed, "There are no changelings. There are only men and women, and betrayal."

Before I hit on the idea of marriage, I plotted for years to acquire a prime gender. One ploy was a memoir. That's the way in, I thought. Memoirists are tattooed with sex; they reek hormones. When people talk about the gulf between memoir and fiction, that's what they mean. It doesn't have much to do with imagination: memoirists make up almost as much stuff as novelists do. The difference is that memoirists stand bowel-deep in the stench of their own creations.

Of course, I'd been writing for years—in lines. Though my body was so long and reedy that on rainy days I was almost two-dimensional, I could still feel the sensation of rocking. But lines did nothing to help me achieve a prime gender. Even hemmed on pages, they distorted scale so wildly, every perception was marred by an infinitesimal vastness.

I pinched my nose, strapped on a tool belt, and pegged *To Prove My Blood* at the top of page one. Meaty stuff, sentences. Their syntax cuts a wide swath. I tried to plow straight but couldn't help a little sway and wobble. Momentarily, the apparitions which animated my rocking would delineate into solid forms, but soon they receded to figures filing through a congruent history. Sentences draped the proscenium of my family's emigration from Ulster to Brooklyn and beyond. I pressed on, drafting my father—how he rumbled through wartime France liberating wine cellars and landed in New York to join the Police Force. At last, I interred the whole family between covers. But no matter how closely I hewed to the brawn of their lives, my sentences still slanted. I never did achieve a prime gender.

Hovering over any memoir is the threat of betrayal. Not just betrayal of family secrets. As an antipersonnel device, a novel can be just as effective. The betrayal consists of translating flesh into sentences. Somehow, lines don't feel so treacherous. Constantly refreshed, they don't pave over the unknowable; they elude the diminishment of scale which results from justified margins. For instance, if Carol Moldaw had written *The Widening* in lines, no one would demand that the identity of the speaker be certified, or wonder how deeply her story paralleled the author's.

Betrayal is a central theme in *The Widening*. Classmates pass scandalous rumors; others leer and snicker. One is reproved with a slap; another expelled from a tryst. The girl feels betrayed by the loss of control over her own depiction. Her body inspires untrustworthy desire. These betrayals coalesce in the second accusation she faces: that she is "privileged."

By most standards, the protagonist *is* privileged: born to wealth, sent to private school, touring Europe before attending Harvard. Yet privilege brings about the deepest betrayal. Joining her daughter on one leg of her Spanish tour, the prim, brittle mother rummages in the girl's backpack and reads her journal. Worse still, she bottles the secret until they return home, where she disgorges the sordid details to her husband, who confronts the heroine with its unsavory revelations.

As a novelistic device, "the journal" is in the changeling Rolodex under "subtext," reminding that *The Widening* is a portrait of the artist as a young woman. The journal is the equivalent of Stephen Dedalus's villanelle on dappled clouds. Of course, the difference is that we hear Stephen's villanelle directly. Scoured of tone and feeling, the girl's journal is reduced to a father's tirade.

But I find myself dwelling on the journal as artifact, not mere device. Was it written in lines? Was it lyrical? Revelatory? Explicit? Does it exist, dormant in an attic of Carol Moldaw's house? I imagine her climbing the stairs at night, retrieving the yellowed pages, rereading words long ago betrayed. Was writing the novel a way of reclaiming the lines of the journal? Is this absent text, of unknown character and depth, the means whereby *The Widening* gains novelistic girth? Is it here that the unnamed central character of the novel and the author, Carol Moldaw, speak as one?

The memoir wasn't my only scheme to gain a prime gender. It's true that my recent marriage is my first, but I've been a father for years, and I have fifty offspring, with more on the way. Prolific? Not really. In the changelings' version of fatherhood, I have become a publisher. We do not conceive, of course, nor watch over birth. Still, in some ways it might be said that we stand at the portal and usher beings into the world.

A year ago, in an airport, with time to kill, I reached into my knapsack for another submission, and pulled out a thin sheaf titled THE WIDENING. By the time I'd finished the manuscript—almost missing my plane—I felt almost embodied, even unique. I was the only stranger who had read this book. And I could act as the agent by which this lost journal and found novel entwined: assisting at the rebirth of lines first betrayed, then redeemed by sentences capable of recalibration, rocking backward, invested with thrum and cadence. That day at the airport, and in many rereadings since that day, whether I begin with chapter one, or open at a random stanza, I felt and feel the nearness of the absent line, the absent journal, and the ineluctably absent—and present—author. I don't care what genre *The Widening* claims. It's the reader, not skin, nor novel or memoir, who finally engulfs.

It's a risky thing to challenge Achebe, the mighty laureate, especially when he speaks for the voiceless against privilege. But don't we all resist reduction to a personal identity? Don't we all hearken to an indeterminate seed? This is the desire which crazes novelists—not to distance themselves from the world, but to plumb their own embryonic core. It's a desire which crazes sentences themselves, causing them to dip backward on their syntactic joints and hinges. No seaworthy sentence lacks rondure.

And *The Widening*—couldn't that title hint at something wider than a single budding womanhood? Could it point toward the dissolution of these provisional boundaries of genre, and even perhaps, boundaries of skin? Maybe it is the widening, not the novel or the memoir, or even the reader, which engulfs. Maybe our desire for embodiment surges backward as well as forward, each arc broadening to dip deeper into the dark. We sentence not merely to embody, or to escape embodiment. Entwined in lines, sentences express our yearning not only to be seen, but to be seen into.

My wife comes from a cove far south of Montauk. She too once stood in the surf, squinting until the horizon forgave its line. Instead of rocking, she sang; giving voice to the myriad tones of sea and sky. Even today, she shivers in the lightest breeze, and if she doesn't pay attention, she lists seaward. But if you heard her sing you'd know why I miss my knees. Her voice may be rocking's *primum mobile.*

We live far from the ocean. And though my gendered incarnation moves in only one direction, I am content. Some restless nights, though, I steal out of our bed and climb the stairs and reach up to the highest attic shelf. I always look behind to be sure I'm safe and alone, then I pull it down—an old knapsack, like the one I imagine contains *The Widening*'s journal. Unknotting the cord, I reach inside up to my elbow, and remove a long sleek skein of sealskin. I unfurl it, run my fingers over the cowl's edge. I bring it to my face and taste the sea. I wrap it around my naked body, and feel the long perfect lines of a body of water. My wife, you see—my beautiful human wife—was born a selkie.

ENGLISH

John Smelcer is an Indian. I am an Irishman. Kyrie Irving is a Celtic. Smelcer has documentation from the Ahtna Native Corporation. I have an Irish passport. Kyrie has a shamrock jersey. In addition to his position as shareholder in Ahtna, Smelcer has blurbs from Norman Mailer, J.D. Salinger, Coretta Scott King, Archbishop Tutu, Chinua Achebe, Noam Chomsky, Ray Bradbury, and the Dalai Lama. I have a trophy from the 1976 All-Ireland basketball tourney. I also sang Clancy Brother songs on family car trips. Kyrie is a flat-earther. He is also skeptical about dinosaurs. "They find one bone," he says, "and make up the rest digitally." On a trek through the Alaskan tundra, Smelcer unearthed the frozen carcass of a woolly mammoth. Unfortunately, he was starving and had to eat the evidence. My mother's pet name was Pet. Pet's favorite song was "Phelim Brady, Bard of Armagh." Many people express shock when they learn that Kyrie Irving believes the earth is flat. He went to Duke, they say. Ahtna, say Native American representatives, is a corporation with shareholders who may or may not be Native American. Pet said to sing my name proud. Smelcer's *Stealing Indians* was named a finalist in the PEN awards. When they finally found out his name, the nomination was rescinded. Phelim is not, finally, Irish for Flip, my pet name. "I have seen a lot of things," says Kyrie, "that my educational system said is real that turns out to be completely fake." Smelcer's second novel won the James Jones First Novel Contest. Then the prize was rescinded. On a car trip, my family left Pet behind at a rest stop. NBA Commissioner Adam Silver says that even though he and Irving attended the same college, they may have taken different classes. Smelcer claims to be the last living speaker of Ahtna. On his website, there is a dictionary and pronunciation guide, and a YouTube clip expounding on Ahtna phonetics. When the Clancys flipped to Irish, I babbled. *An poc ar buille. Óró sé do bheatha abhaile. Gile na gile.* Silver says that he believes Irving was "trying to be provocative." The chair of the James Jones Award Committee says, "We took him off the website because he's an embarrassment to us." When *Phantom Signs* went to Universe City, one anonymous reader flipped the bird at the rhetorical question, "Who wants to read an essay on race by a pale-faced junior geezer?" Duke's Kyrie Irving web page displays thirty-one bullet points, including his Australian birth and his pet's name, without one mention of class. Marlon James, who graduated from Wilkes University where Smelcer taught briefly before being released, says he is "a living con job." In English, the Clancy Brothers sang gibberish, but in West Cork I strayed out of Bandon, passed Clonakilty, and delayed at Ballinascarthy just like in the song, which I hummed in the empty rental. Flat-earthers are Truthers, believing, says the English dictionary, that "an important subject or event is being concealed from the public by a powerful conspiracy." Released, *Phantom Signs* may flip the name "Trump" for the name "Smelcer." Kyrie Irving may flip to "Kobe Bryant" or, with opposite spin, "Steve Francis." "I" could flip to "Incomplete." Anonymous sources say, "Kyrie doesn't want to be treated like LeBron's son." Smelcer's adoptive father says, "He's a blond, blue-eyed Caucasian, just like anyone else." After her death, I found Pet's docs, listing place of birth as Motherwell, Scotland; not, as she'd always claimed, Armagh. Kyrie's Pepsi commercial alter-ego is a junior geezer, "Uncle Drew." Smelcer says his father is trying to "publicly destroy his son." If Phelim is not Flip I am not sung. Flat-earthers are not Birthers, but both flip off truth. Based on his Native American birth, Smelcer was hired at the University of Alaska. Then he was rescinded. A Ballinascarthy barman thumbed a shamrock on my Beamish head—just messing, he says. James must have messed with Kyrie's head. On his website, Smelcer says he used "careful wording during the hiring process. The question was never put to me, point blank, 'Are you a full-blood Indian?' I was very careful with the dictionary, finding that word 'affiliated.' After all," says Smelcer, "I was an English major." The anonymous reader flipped out at *Phantom Signs*. Flat-earthers believe nothing they can't see. *The Kenyon Review* published two Smelcer poems. Then publication was rescinded. According to Irish baby names, Phelim means "Good Forever," whereas the urban dictionary says "Weirdo with very thing [*sic*] eyebrows, sunbed [*sic*] skin, very strange hairstyle that drinks a lot and drives home the next day still over the limit like an absolute wanker." Kyrie says, "If someone didn't teach you you were spinning on a ball orbiting the Sun, is that what you observe with your senses?" "We believed John Smelcer," says a university spokesman, "to be an Alaska Native at the time of the hire." Three songs after forgetting Pet we missed her. Two songs later we turned back. Kyrie has been traded to the Boston Celtics. In Queens, Boston is taboo, but I loved shamrocks. On his website, Smelcer has posted a defense. He is traduced; his stepfather is his father; the faculty at the University of Alaska are mean; Native American critics misunderstand; the PEN and Jones committees and Wilkes administration and *Kenyon* editors hate real writers. The anonymous reader would not sign off on *Phantom Signs*. Kyrie spun everything to be released from James. Does rescinding Smelcer release us? There are things that cannot be released, and this is the drive and reason for *Phantom Signs,* and for all literature, and for the spinning orb. Kyrie Irving has the sweetest English in the game, but he has never released his transcripts. Playing in Ireland, I signed autographs "Rick Barry." Do Trump's hands flatten belief? Kyrie's release could have left him anywhere—Phoenix. Sacdo. Deathlyn. Sherman Alexie says, "I just want to go on the record, in case I unexpectedly die, that I never read a book by Smelcer." Kyrie says he wanted to be himself alone. Ourselves alone is English for *Sinn Fein;* ergo, Kyrie is a terrorist. Debbie Reese says, "His representations of his own identity are a mess. His writing is a mess." The anonymous reader may have been expending final effort against spin, and could spare no hand against more English. *Sports Illustrated* says, "Can what one senses discredit what mathematics proves?" Anonymously, Smelcer was himself alone. Named, he was rescinded. After the anonymous reader checked "No," under *Publish,* Universe City named another reader; ergo *Phantom Signs* is released into your hands. In the fourth quarter of game seven of the 2016 NBA finals, during the greatest comeback in earth's history, Irving spun from Klay Thompson, stutter-stepped, and dove to the hole, where he wrong-footed his leap and flipped from his left hip an orb which lofted just over the outstretched hand of fellow flat-earther Draymond Green, was released from gravity, and re-entered earth's pull, kissing the glass beyond the left upper corner of the square with the exact English to complete the perfect angle and fall, as Kyrie landed, through hoop and net. Nothing past that English do I truth.

PART
4

THE MUSE IN UNIVERSE CITY

NINE PHANTOM SIGNS

GAY

Not gay. Gay. Yeats's gay. Their glittering eyes were gay, gay. Poised between worlds. Flensed of fear and lust. Joyous not merry. Grave not sad. There is no other word for this condition. When it left, did its sense vanish? Were we made binary? Am I now wholly not gay?

I started out gay. Smooth as an egg, I was so bendable I could kiss my toes. On winter Sunday mornings, I snuck down to the basement and stripped, admiring bone and flesh, angle of toe and knuckle, cant of head, each surface devising its own signature. Nude, I burst into the snow—a dash which would not have terrified if it were into pasture or fen or Burren and not a postage stamp under the spider eyes of row house windows.

Maybe everyone starts out gay, in both species of the word. The body is other. It is another. It is wonder.

I am not gay, but of the fourteen eyes which have desired me, eight belonged to men. The Irish poet wanted to cuddle. The Prep coach flecked spittle in his shower tirades. And a pair of ABDs from the college of éclat introduced me to oysters and Al Jarreau and Glenfiddich. Theirs was a world of silk scarves and first editions and Marxist gossip.

"Why not try?" they purred.

Never had I fancied sex so civilized, but the more inviting their invitation, the more diffident I became.

My first crush was a boy at camp. Fearless, I call him in my phantom sign, and I dove deeper into love than in real life. In life Fearless and I drifted in day-dreamed boats, and at night in the sign we read by the light of our wet skin.

> From dappled green a dazzling white unstrangled.
> Fearless emerged naked from the sea.
> Naked he washed each night into my bed.
> Naked I drowned face down in burning white.

And mornings as Odysseus hectored,
I witnessed Fearless blinking in his bunk
Across the room as if he'd never braved
The night crossing decorously composed
In the alabaster body of a ship.

I did not choose not to be gay. Straightness was visited upon me. It was a falling away. No longer could I moon over Fearless, or sprint invisibly through my yard. Girls remained veiled. The entire gender was sequestered behind rows of bolted desks and unwinnable games and furious giggles. For many years straight, I addressed no object of desire.

Straightness was a metamorphosis: I became tall. Once smooth and bendable, my body elongated while resisting girth until my chest caved in and the fingers of one hand could encircle a thigh. My ears unhinged. The cartilaginous right speared like an antler, the left lobe drooped below the jaw. Eyelids pinked. Lashes crusted. The trunk roiled, mapping new pustules. Bloody pus spotted morning sheets.

My height was a phenomenon. Passersby gawked. I towered over cops and nuns. I lumbered down asphalt courts while hobbits dribbled around my knees. I delivered canned speeches in schoolboy contests and was often mistaken for the moderator. Only once was I touched by unbent love.

At Rockaway, under the Ferris wheel, a shriek pierced the Easter air, and a cool body wriggled up my back, arms wrapping my neck. Warm lips wetted my cheek. It was no dream, I lay broad waking. Then a scream. I was not him—the boyfriend she'd embraced from behind. That moment stayed—and harkened. Parts of me resembled parts of someone who was loved. From certain angles, it was possible to love me. I decided to continue to be tall.

Meanwhile, behind the spider eyes of the row houses, gay warped into queer, homo, fag. Yeats was nowhere. Sometimes gay hovered just beyond the text. One evening Mother came home from night class puzzled because her handsome English professor had outed the protagonist of Willa Cather's "Paul's Case." Mother didn't mind that Paul was gay, but why not say? Sad, yes. But why gay? Why do writers hide words? Why do professors impose them?

If I were gay I might impose myself.

"My Lady," I would pirouette, "Why are you unfree to gaze at this?"

"How signal lust," I'd importune, "without permission to shout Booyah! or honk your car horn or stick out your tongue or flick a cigarette lighter or unzip?" Platonically, I'd inquire, "How many adjustments, and what kind, would this body need to make to be desired?"

And finally, as I sipped from demitasse, "How, August Vision, do you conceal eternal truth in every beauteous step?"

Imposing makes me see I don't mean gay. I mean gay. I mean not acting or being acted upon, but apprehending in sublimity. If gay means only gay, the world splits to binary. Metaphors flatten. Thought congeals to doctrine. Syntax straightens out.

Whatever orientation, Yeats's eyes belonged to figurines. Fictional Paul lives twice in the unsaid word. He is not sad but grave. Paul's glittering eyes are Cather's gay.

A time came when my height was less phenomenal. Other features emerged: Woodstock hair and a bandito moustache. Also, the hobbits had caught up. In fact, among hoopsters I was virtually short. Upon this figure fell the gaze of the second beauty to desire me.

By day she was a Greek professor, by night a sea nymph. How we came to be alone in her apartment I don't know. I was twenty; she, millennia older. Reclining on her divan in her living room with gilt-framed prints and seashells and wine bottles and a Persian rug, she told me that once, she had rebuffed advances from my poetry prof, a homunculus whose brilliance was Homeric.

"Why me?" I stuttered, "And not him."

Her heavy-lidded eyes drank in my flesh.

"If you were him we'd be in bed," she said.

Then we were.

Never had I seen a naked woman. Pieces yes, revealed, suggested. And everywhere, iconic representations: graffiti that looked like paramecia. A peach splash pierced with centerfold staples. Shadows undulating on frat walls.

But this. Encompassing, unveiled. The lip of sea and sky blurring to cleft. And at the vortex, the glistening ruby tympanum inverted. Lifting my curls I shimmied down past the spangled breasts, deeper to the navel and beneath, the gateway to being and regression.

Long ago in Health class a lab rat had chalked a horned bull's head.

"Cervix," he had pointered. "Fallopian tubes."

But here was no depiction. My head was clasped between the sea nymph's thighs. No graffiti, porn, or diagram could manifest this delta, this climate, an ecosystem of dismaying breadth, too long for one upsweep of the tongue, fringed in profuse hair thinning toward the tawny puck of deeper pungency—a separate region, and yet borderless. No boy examining his flesh, and flesh of other pimply boys in gym, could ever have inferred such a landscape: its rasp, its vibrancy, its bruised stigma, its centrifugal force, its implications.

Fully engulfed, I plunged between palisades and past the portico into the very pith of the Pergamon. The upheaval of her ululating cry lasted an instant. Gravity held her body by one heel.

"This is it," I thought, thus erasing it.

"Don't screw up," I thought, thus doing so.

Then I was alone on a windy beach, shipwrecked beneath the stars, and when my eyes finally spun open I saw my office for the years to come: to elegize the distance to this echoing absence.

The last person ever to desire me stood on a sidewalk in Youngstown, Ohio, outside the Unitarian church after the wedding of two friends. The recessional piped. Guests milled. Fall clouds drifted overhead.

As I knotted my silk scarf, I caught sight of a beauty, hair braided, green eyes playful. Her lyrical mezzo voice rippled the air. "There's a dashing man."

I turned to look behind. But no one followed. It was me. This was what I had become. In that double-take I glimpsed the gay child naked in the snowy yard and the gay man dying in the sea nymph's arms. They didn't know that all the time they had been destined for this. What could I do?

Reader, I married her.

HEX

There is a word that I am loathe to say. It sends a small shiver up my spine. Not the usual—fuck, cunt, shit, prick, ass. Nor the sloppy ones like darling, pumpkin, sweetie pie, lambkins. Hearing "Yaddo" always made a friend wrinkle her nose, but I lack allergies to odd-sounding words like firkin or Iroquois. I pronounce with equanimity terms that portend evil, like triglycerides. I am not dismissive of tongue twisters or ululation or jaw harping. I jabber to my cat. I sing alone.

It's just this one word. It does not relate to sex, exactly, though one of its definitions is a body part. I would not say it out loud to myself, or to others if I could safely circumlocute. I would not have it uttered within earshot. The French version doesn't squick me, which is ironic since the English is an obscenity in French. It is not a fetish; it does not fester behind a veil of incense and fishhooks. Though I can write the word, to write it while admitting that I would not say it—this I cannot.

I hex this word. I do not curse or swear. I hex it. If I spoke my hexed word you would not cringe. It is not shameful. But to say that I cannot say it would color my humanity; it would divide us, reader, in this particular. Hex is the lust of virgin silence, the tensing of the unfired synapse, the spell between bars of the equal sign. Hex causes and precedes. Sans hex, words perfectly denote. They mean the same to everyone. They lack gaiety.

Every utterance is spun, like a charmed quark, by its hex. If all my hexes were perfectly aligned with Yeats's, I would have composed "Lapis Lazuli." Maybe I did. Loopy hexes spat out a book-length tale in blank verse. It zigzagged between myth and time. It opened with a list of everything that happens and does not. On the cover, it says *To Banquet with the Ethiopians: A Memoir of Life Before the Alphabet.* The name beneath is the same as the name beneath these words. Usually, it's bad form to talk about one's own book, but it's OK here because it did not sell very much and if my name is on the dust jacket, it is only because none other has stepped forward.

The 265th item on the list of everything and not reads simply, "Thersites." So in my phantom sign, that is my name. Telemachus is my father. Homer is a novice scrivener. Fearless is a perfect gay child who lived inside my body and Odysseus and Achilles and Agamemnon are counselors at a summer camp for boys.

> The heroes of Thersites' beach camp
> Were Agamemnon, Achilles, and Odysseus.
> And so were the heroes of my beach camp.
> I named them from the paperback I'd nicked
> From a bin outside the Main Street 5&10.
> "A Great Adventure Story," it was billed.
> "The Greatest War Novel Ever Penned."
> Perched on a spavined bunk I clutched the book
> And when Achilles or Odysseus
> Or royal Agamemnon strode by,
> I buried my nose till pages came unglued.

Before my book dissolved to my phantom sign it was composed of sentences. Stong and regular, they pulsed across the page, right justified, chapter upon paragraph. Then one autumn afternoon deep in midlife, there was a numbness in the syntax, a dependent clause cracked and then, an explosion.

> I died, I think. It could be
> A child's fingers trace the livid script—
> A cave figure or totem. It could be
> My stitched chest is a chirograph
> Metastasizing into memoir.
> Thus my body, transcribed, rocks
> Backward, washed clean of birth,

Forward into days charted by lines,
Backward like a wave or a half rhyme
And forward into the summer of 265
When I first bent solemn to the page.

The sentences were no longer mine. They were no longer sentences. They were pent up. But they were still colored by my hex. Otherwise they might be "Lapis Lazuli."

PENT

Bribed or threatened, I might yield up a hex I have outgrown.

When I was young, it signified constraint: gram, gon, x, teuch, angle. It conjured cop cars, chastity, titration. Pented, one—distinct from two—always left three. Pent meant suicides: foul line, half, three quarters, full, again. It was five boroughs I could not escape. Five segments of the Latin Mass. It was school togs: shoes, belt, pressed pants, starched shirt, tie. It notched degrees of separation from the feminine. Poetry was pent—Keats, Wordsworth, Milton, Tennyson, Pope: da DA, da DA, da DA, da DA, da DA. Everything pent always as was pent.

One day I overstepped the spider-eyed row houses and ventured on windy plains where I met Protestants and bell-bottoms and seven footers and a sea nymph, and in my wanderings by motorbike and Greyhound and blue boogey I met specimens who declared that they themselves wrote verse.

How so? I thought, when they were not deceased. Poets, they claimed to be, though the world called them barflies, waitresses, potheads, earth mothers, and Buddhists. Some were addled. Two saw God. One wore black. None walked lonely as a cloud. All were religiously unpent.

Since poets were extant, I thought I might become one. I enrolled at the University of Delaware to sit at the feet of the Parnassians rented by Zack Bowen, ex-used-car-salesman and understudy for Falstaff, with dash siphoned from DuPont's napalm funding. These were the high nabobs of verse. Bespangled and priapic, they glided down corridors, never touching a doorknob. Some copped feels and guzzled through receptions. One attempted Jesuitics. A few politely absented themselves from the sublunary.

Yet, all had once been pent. "My name is James A. Wright and I was born," one had begun. All his early volumes—*The Green Wall* and *Saint Judas*—were pent. But by the time of his term in Newark—the year before his death—his lines were breaking into blossom.

> Murdered, I went, risen
> where the murderers are,
> that black ditch
> of river.

Galway Kinnell, that saturnine bear, recited on his haunches while a dancing flower-child peeled off her blouse. But he too had once been pent.

> It was now fine music the frogs and the boy
> Did in the towering Illinois twilight make

Flaccid in person, Kinnell's page had tensed and fractured, unpent.

> Until one day I totter and fall—
> fall on this
> stomach that has tried so hard to keep up,
> to digest the blood as it leaked in,
> to break up

Even W. D. Snodgrass, whiskered as Henry Pussycat, was de-penting, if more slowly, weighed down by the Pulitzer hung around the neck of his first book. Their late lines were unpent, but not their flesh. If they yearned for their bodies to break into blossom, it was *their* bodies they yearned to break. Their lines were their signature; every crack hexed.

It was not Wright or Snodgrass or Kinnell who unpent me. It was Mother. In the years between Rockaway and the night my gay self perished in the sea nymph, I had tried everything to squirm out of straight tallness: gothic novels, rosaries, Boone's Farm, cock-spasming. Mostly, I rocked, back and forth, in front of the cabinet hi-fi, listening to Father's Clancy Brothers records babble from another world.

On hands and knees, speed adjusted to song, I rocked. But however long and far, always I stayed pent outside the music, inside the row house. Finally, I begged Mother to take me back, show me the place I'd come from.

"Ah you whelp. I can't, I'd be ashamed. And it's too small to see, covered with hair."

That image made Father's clinical explanation seem savage, and filled me with terror no rocking could soothe. I feared we were separately pent in our own row houses or five boroughs or misshapen flesh. I feared I would live forever. That's what sent me out on the windy plain. When I started to compose myself,

I thought the zigzag walk might be my exit and so I tore and cut and radically enjambed, to break miraculously into blossom.

Wright, Kinnell, and Snodgrass have all since bloomed, but then we were alive, pent up, and saw no avenue out but splintered lines.

The sea nymph did not offer a way out but back inside. Immersed in her gossamer bed—yes, there was that—but first, in her day job. The Greek prof gave me hope I might repent.

On the blackboard beneath the proscenium she chalked, "Hexameter is the sea's utterance."

I stared from the back row at the undulating surf of her panty line as she announced that Homer was the first and last poet to share his meter with everyone, because he lived and did not live.

"Analysts say many Homers," she scrawled. "Unitarians, 1."

I followed the undulation of her sea-borne breasts.

"The mode of composition, the multiform, the traditional referentiality, the echoic resonance, claim Analysts, demonstrate the multiplicity of sources."

"Nine Greek cities claim birth," I copied. "Others say H not from Greece at all."

The sea nymph twerked to the blackboard and I scribbled, "H's Trojan sympathies—came from Troy?

"Homer>Homeros>Hostage."

"Some scholars," said the sea nymph, now perched on the oak desk with a wingéd sandal dangling from her toe, "invent etymologies. Iman Jacob Wilkens claims that the confluence of rivers in England so match Homer's description that Troy must be located in Cambridgeshire. Edo Nyland says Homer spoke a version of ancient Basque.

"On the other hand," her upturned palm mapped joy, "Unitarians cite the novelistic structure: Opening as a bildungsroman, the *Odyssey* introduces themes that climax far later in the poem—distances which no single performance could traverse. There are the shifting perspectives; the way the text speaks to text. There are the unresolved endings. The flashbacks. The complex relationships to the Trojans. The fact that Achilles, a late interpolation, is the only character with folkloric associations—raised by a centaur, cross-dressing, gifted with talking horses. All these clues argue for a single Homeric voice."

From the cheap seats a blank hand spasmed up.

"But mizz," it whined. "Which is it?"

The sea nymph gazed into the wine-dark rows.

"Homer," she said, "is Homeros and Numerous. He is Melesigines. He is

Achilles and Odysseus and Thersites and Elpenor and Aeneus and Satan and Humphrey Chimpden Earwicker. He is flesh composed of text. His Muse is one in many. Many in one. He is everyone and no one."

I couldn't keep up. My untouched hand cramped. Finally, I gave up note-taking and listened.

"Embedded in each line, said the sea nymph, "is the undertow and climax of the entire poem."

She skimmed across the stage. I heard over and over "climax" and "embedded" and remembered lust's undertow, unpent.

"To the ancients," she said, "every epic was Homeric: The *Cypria,* the *Aethiopis,* the *Iliupersis* the *Nostoi* and the *Telegony*—all Homer's. And his father, says the oracle, was spawned from Homer's own text—Odysseus's son, Telemachus."

One husband, one church, two children, and a cluster of spider-eyed neighbors pent Mother, but on her deathbed, she whispered that she was going back to the place she came from, the source she could not until then reveal. That day, I knew I had not really died in the sea nymph. And when the surgeon Xed my heart out of my body, I did not go home. I could not rock. I could not hex in the meter of the ocean. My hexes are imperfectly aligned. My hexameter is truncated by a word I cannot bear. I can trace only one phantom sign, like this.

> Step one: be born. The hind foot pairs,
> Pirouettes, kicks, uncouples.
> Foot three: the chirograph unseals.
> Toes cleave to cliff, printing blood
> Over a deep caesura. Many fall.
> Others turn back. But those who bridge
> With elevated speech to the pent-
> Ultimate foot—the psychostasia—
> They weigh hearts. Having stepped
> Into my chest, the fourth foot
> Finds me light—flensed of fear and lust.
> My palpitations begin to coalesce
> Into mortal cadence. πε√τε,
> The last step knows it is last. Is not
> Redeemable by surf or sky.
> It faces down the margin, quavers slightly.
> Beyond the fifth—nothing.
> The blank page aching to be born.

POET

The closest I can come to the hexed word that I will not write is to say that

1. it is the means whereby sound and silence are organized into meter
2. it has been truncated from hex to pent
3. it slant rhymes with poet.

Poet is another hex that I am willing to reveal though it is heavy laden. It's not outmoded, like troubadour or rhapsode. Still, it emits a whiff of absurdity, like haven or nought. It does not exist on the same plane as carburetor, cheeseburger, or snot.

Behind every Eng. Dept. office door lurks a poet. In every bottom drawer, an unfinished ode. Since poetry unlike prose has no predetermined parts, everyone yearns to fill it with themselves. Those who claim that they began as readers with no pretense to make versions of what they read have suppressed their origins. No curate on this corridor—not the comp coordinator nor the medievalist nor the theory guru nor the IT dweeb—no one did not at one time harbor the fantasy, or even cultivate the ambition, of being a poet.

Nor does this folly end with Eng. Depts. Anyone touched by a poem burns to write one—or better, to have written. This is not true of novels or plays or screenplays or memoirs. Like acrobatics or opera, I love to watch, but do not seek to emulate. But poems look easy; they make us feel we too could ignite language. As a provost once asked, "Is that a real poem or did you just make it up?"

In the end, almost everyone turns from the hex to the world, where they might do some good. Those who do not turn away are not necessarily the most gifted, they are merely the most stubborn—and this fact irks some readers who settled for less exalted vocations, prompting quips: "Get your wax out of the sun, Ic'rus," and "Let's not let the animals run the zoo."

In the hex, poets find a burden and a haven. The haven is a place no one will touch which they themselves have made. The burden? What to do with the twenty-three hours a day one is not making a poem.

Take for instance Theodore Roethke's beloved *Collected Poems*, and divide its five thousand lines by the thirteen thousand days during which Roethke published. There is of course no actual timetable. He punched no clock. Ted was on call 312,000 hours. Like firefighters or lighthouse keepers, poets have many days of nought. No gyre widening. Not even a little bush burning. It's taxing—standing tiptoe on a peak gripping a lightning rod, shushing the wind. In fact, maintaining the idea of being a poet during all those hours makes poets wobble slightly whenever they touch down. It's why, when a poet tells the cop or plumber or cabbie or provost her profession, an eyebrow cocks. It's why the Irish poet said, "Poet is not a title to confer upon oneself. It is," he sniffed, "an honorific." It's why Snodgrass told us not to be poets "If you can be happy doing anything else." It's why Kinnell said that the salient characteristics of American poets were "stubbornness and stupidity, lighted with genius."

If you've got twenty-three hours, why not write novels on the side? Make some spondulicks. Grab some fame. There have been some: Graves, Atwood, Moldaw, Stein, Loy. But the fact that so few poets write novels and the few novelists who write poetry look like Michael Jordan in the batting cage suggests some difference at the core of these identities. Not just alternative conventions or processes. But what it means to be . . . nought.

Novels are written by novelists. Memoirs by memoirists. Plays by playwrights. But poets are not ists. They do not wright. To be present, they absent themselves. Poised on the border of nought, they listen. Though the Muse is silent, they attend. Though there is nothing out there, they forget everything but. And absence takes time. Twenty-three hours a day, on average.

This is where Universe City comes in—a haven that further weights the burden. Don't get me wrong, I love Universe City. The quads, the libraries, the chimes, the demonstrations and jargon and flying mortarboards and dancing mascots. At Universe City, the young stay young forever and the seminar never sets. In fact, Universe City has made poetry lucrative. When Gotham scriveners brag of fat advances, or Hollywood screenwriters gossip about celebrities, I shake my head.

"There's a company," I tell them, "that pays a civil service salary for six years if they like your first book."

That gives them pause.

"It doesn't even have to sell well."

That stops their gallop.

"All you have to do," I say, "is move to whatever podunk burg they pick and do two days a week community service."

That sets their wigs on fire.

"And if they like your second book," I tap their chests, "they'll give you that deal for life."

"What company?" they demand.

"Universe City," I deadpan.

Who wouldn't want this gig? Competition is fierce. An MFA is just a ticket to the MLA; you better be packing an NEA or Guggenheim or NBA or Pulitzer or Kingsley Tufts or Juniper or Fulbright or at least one of the junior versions. Fresh faced, in their parents' brogues or pearls, the acolytes tender CV's gothed up with prizes and encomia. But when the anointed ones pass through the ivy-covered portal and strap on to the tenure track, they become poets all twenty-four hours. Sitting on committees, they are poets. Scrolling through budgets, they are poets. They are teaching poets and advising poets and bargaining unit poets and distinguished chair poets. The poems themselves are anthologized and peer reviewed and sabbaticalated.

"A novelist," says Henry James, "is someone upon whom nothing is lost." But poets lean over the border of nought, right at the vortex of forgetting. Poetry isn't written; it is the impression left after everything not a poem has dissolved. Being a poet as an occupation, with semesters and promotion documents and assessment tools and banner numbers, makes forgetting very, very hard.

Under the eyes of the towers of Universe City, poets read and re-read and edit and redact until each utterance hardens into prose. There is no silence between lines or within words. Nought is beaten into not—the diphthong and orthographic antiquity smoothed over. There is no hex. The layering of utterance over silence flattens out.

Universe City shifts the burden of visibility from poem to poet. Personal identity is never not seen; it cages each poem; the opus is netted in an oeuvre. For nought, the poet seeks another haven.

Some try blending in. "I have eaten the plums which you left on the refrigerator and were probably saving for breakfast."

Some densify. "The force that through the green fuse drives the flower."

Some spiral into iconoclasm. "When gong and conch declare the hour to bless, Grimalkin crawls to Buddha's emptiness."

Some vanish at differing rates of speed. "Oh quickly disappearing photograph in my more slowly disappearing hand."

But Universe City sees through the vernacular and texture and obfuscation and flux. Instead of nought, there stand the pinstriped autographs of Williams and Thomas and Yeats and Rilke.

Universe City filters out utterance and transliterates nought directly into sign. The more poetry written, the more prosaic. What confounds a poet in Universe City isn't fatigue or bandwidth, it is the absence of the chthonic otherness beneath their feet.

For instance, who would remember this tiny fragment if it were not scrawled in the margin of the ninth-century Book of St. Gallen?

> The sea is wild tonight.
> No need to fear

> that Viking hordes will come
> and terrify me.

It's not only the Vikings which terrify, but the strange immediacy of midnight, the tallowy hand, the coarse-spun robe and frosty breath of the Hiberian monk who defaced the elegantly calligraphied margins of the codex he illuminated. Bashō's haiku, which seem a moment's thought, are sustained by the frame of elegant haiga. Beneath Dante's Italian purrs two thousand years of Latin, and Eliot's jazz riffs off Donne and Wyatt. Form comes to life when utterance strikes eternity, revealing for an instant cosmic scale, a vast midnight landscape illuminated by lightning.

How can such lightning flash and darken when Universe City produces volumes to produce poets to produce students to produce volumes? Every year thousands of sixty-four-page monographs are ISBN'ed and blurbed and liked. They do not exist, exactly—except as CV lines and InDesign programs and Amazon web pages. But their myriad titles pave over nought a metropolis of print.

If an atom were expanded to the size of the earth, physicists say, the nucleus would be the size of a cherry and electrons would still be microscopic. Physicists are gay. The solid world is not solid. To reveal cosmic scale, poetry must radically dislocate the earth. Prose is an illusion nought dispels.

NOUGHT

The first poet to come to nought was Homer. In his wanderings, he encountered two Universe Cities—places so exotic they seemed, to this bog-trotting bard fresh from the dark ages, like other worlds.

First, Troy. Unlike the Argive dropouts barbecuing on the beach, the Trojans are cultured and cosmopolitan. Priam is grave and judicious; Hector, a brash lad in touch with his feminine side. While Argive conclaves degenerate into brawls, the Trojan assemblies are civilized. Yet, like any department meeting, Troy's councils take place in the penumbra of a great crime which their urbanity is powerless to mitigate. As for their poets—Cassandra they drown out, and Laocoön they just drown.

Meanwhile, the hero deepest into nought is the least collegial.

> They came to the ships and huts of the Myrmidons.
> There they found Achilles. He was easing his spirit
> with a tuneful finely decorated lyre.
> It had a silver cross-piece. He'd seized it as a prize

when he'd destroyed the city of Eëtion.
With the lyre he was bringing pleasure to his heart,
singing about the celebrated deeds of men.

Achilles sings history on an instrument wrested from the war he sings. The scene speaks to a self-awareness that sharpens when sign separates from utterance, and the poet begins to count the twenty-three hours a day of not writing. The same mirroring of fiction and reality occurs in the *Odyssey*, when Demodocus sings about Odysseus to Odysseus in the second Universe City, Phaeacia.

The minstrel was inspired by the Muse to sing
a song about the glorious deeds of warriors,
that tale, whose fame had climbed to spacious heaven . . .

Odysseus' strong hands took his purple cloak,
pulled it above his head, and hid his handsome face.
He felt ashamed to let Phaeacians look at him
with tears streaming from his eyes.

Critics often see Demodocus as Homer's stand-in. He sings of Odysseus; he knows the epic even as events unfold. It looks like a Hitchcock cameo. But it's staged. Homer isn't portraying the act of communing with the Muse; this isn't inspiration. Odysseus, not Calliope, decides where and how to start.

"Come, change the subject now and sing about
the building of that wooden horse, the one
Epeius made with guidance from Athena.
Lord Odysseus then, with his trickery
had it brought to the citadel, filled with men,
those who ransacked Troy. If, at my request,
you will recite the details of this story,
I'll tell all men how, of his own free will,
god gives poetic power to your song."

Odysseus the recruit solicits Demodocus to sing Odysseus the alumnus so that Odysseus the provost can raise funds. If the poet plays along, Odysseus the publisher will blurb. Odysseus the trustee will confer an honorarium he telethoned from a benefactor, like any good nonprofit.

At Odysseus' words, the herald took the serving
and handed it to noble Demodocus
who accepted it with a delighted heart.

Outside Universe City poetry doesn't work like this. It doesn't begin and end. It isn't directed or judged. It isn't a signed broadsheet. It doesn't win prizes. It doesn't get paid. It doesn't exclude all that doesn't appear on the page.

At the gates of Universe City, Homer stood in awe. But touring the campus, he started to sweat; his tinnitus ratcheted up; his knees clicked. Behind the teichoscopia, he glimpsed Priam's venality, Paris's cupidity, the callowness of Hector. They believed their own eloquence, ignoring the silence of the gods. They schemed and prevaricated and cajoled, right down to bargaining the number of days for Hector's funeral. In the end, Homer declined to matriculate. With an SDS fist pump, he let Troy burn, baby, burn.

Then, for a lifetime, he went silent, drowned in nought. Fifty years, scholars say, passed between the composition of the two surviving Homeric epics.

At the opening of the *Iliad*, making verse had been natural. Utterance was inspired.

"Sing, Goddess, Achilles's rage," and you're off.

But writing is hard. You can sing till breathless, but writing requires more exacting choices. He penned the *Cypria*, the *Aethiopis*, the *Iliupersis* the *Nostoi* and the *Telegony*. But each line transcribed out of the air hardened into prose. At the end, Homer deleted every file.

Refracting utterance onto the page demanded so much time and yielded so little song, Homer's eyes blurred and his hands trembled. Stale coffee, noisy neighbors, barking dogs, Gauloises, and ouzo. Everything tilted, swelled, then shriveled to letters. Twenty-three hours expanded to nine years of war, then shrank to fifty days of fighting. The *Nostoi* he had drafted and torn up braided into a single tale. A decade of Cyclops, Hades, Laestrygonians, Circe, Aeolus, and Cattle of the Sun redacted into four chapters folded into twenty-four.

Homer fought back. He strove to render utterance on the page. In common parlance, no one would say "nought," any more than "rosy-fingered" or "swift-footed" or "many-minded" or "earth-thundering." Homer kept them in anyway, just where they would have once been sung. And more. Homer hexed the page, using the ancient multiforms: the arming of the hero, marshaling troops, feasting and sailing of ships and single combat; he laid out each of the six beats of the sea's utterance in a language that had never been spoken in prose. But still he could not find his footing. No longer could he command the Muse to start here or there. He could only beg, opening the *Odyssey*, "Muse, begin anywhere you will."

By the time he reached Phaeacia, Homer had emerged from the sea of utterance into the haven of the chirographic world, bearing a burden: an individuated self, with a point of view and name and rank. He was a poet, with twenty-three hours of nought. Homer had no patience for an assistant professor crooning for tenure. It squicked him. He rubbed out Demodocus and let Odysseus tell his tale in his own words in the first ever fictive first-person narration. Is Odysseus Homer? Is his story true? Get real.

If not Demodocus, then who? Hostage? Trojan refugee? Son of the son of his own protagonist? Spaniard? Brit? Yank?

Nought. Not confined to one incarnation. Homer is no single person any more than the Muse is one entity. He is everyone and no one, as the Muse is the hinge between utterance and sign.

Meanwhile, book jackets yearned for a big name. They snatched Homer. Then they shoved a boulder down the throat of the Universe City of Phaeacia so no new name could get back in or out.

HAVEN

A book launches a thousand e-mails. There is production and design and marketing and copyediting and proofing and budgeting and interning and soothing and redesign and clarifying and accounting and pre-sales and sales. Therefore, we at Etruscan Press assign each new release a phantom sign—especially useful for long titles. *A Heaven Wrought of Iron* is Haven.

Today Haven arrived by mail. Not a book—though it resembles a book in all things but the red stamp: Uncorrected Proof. This is as close to a book as Homer ever got, or Joyce for years and years. They threw up their hands. My hands are on the phantom sign; it feels real, but it is not a book. The cover is matte, not gloss, and the Pantone greenish. They say that POD matches offset, but I still find galleys a tad flimsy. The blurbs are not right justified and the author pic is low-res, and the PCIP has not been checked. I could not vouch for the line breaks, or for the geography of stanzas, which emerge from recycled, acid-free, uncoated white like chirographic archipelagoes.

I did not write this book. And somehow, neither did the author, though we—that is, the publishers—have branded D. M. Spitzer on the cover and in all the conventional places in the interior. I have not met D. M. Spitzer. I did not know his name until Haven came over the transom. I verified his existence with a phone call. He seems like a nice guy.

Haven is a long poem that is also a poetic reading of the *Odyssey*. It is not criticism, or commentary, or pastiche. A companion, perhaps. A new rendering, in the mode of Alice Oswald's *Memorial* and Zachary Mason's *The Lost Books of the Odyssey* and Chris Logue's *War Music*. I loved it at first reading. It felt immediate, yet arrived from a far place—maybe an ancient blog excavated near Hisarlik, Anatolia.

All the words in the book are translated from, adopted from, or inspired by Greek originals. The *Odyssey* is therefore Haven's hex, though I presume that Haven's English would be oblique to Homer, who in any case was blind and lived before the alphabet; so English would have been the least of his problems. But the words, seen or withheld, belong to Homer.

Until its publication, when it becomes *A Heaven Wrought of Iron*, Haven is strange and precious. It is rare—copies only for the author, staff, a few friends, and reviewers. It may yet change; it is a living thing, organic and frangible. It is visibly unseen. It is a book and it is nought.

Does Haven belong to Homer or to Spitzer? Or to me, who will monitor its birth?

"Hold on," says Haven.

> Remember: forget.
> Hide yourself from yourself.
> Remember: forget.

Meanwhile,

> Periphrastically
> expectation
> turned into my name.

The sea nymph said that Homer was every poet's hex, but who was Homer's? Did expectation turn into his name?

Homer did not invent his names. They are not fictional. Achilles was son of Peleus and father of Neoptolemus; Odysseus was son of Laertes and father of Telemachus; Hector was son of Priam and father of the unfortunate Astyanax. They walked the earth before Homer inscribed their deeds.

Only three characters are made up. These are the only figures with no patronymics, no lineage that places both feet on earth. Their existence depends wholly on the text in which their signs appear. Just as there would be no Haven without *A Heaven Wrought of Iron*, so these three characters would not exist without the *Iliad* and the *Odyssey*. They are not burdened by mortality. We do not know their birthplace. We do not know what becomes of them, except by the accounts of the poems.

The first fictional character is Homer. Nine Greek cities claim his birth. He may be one person, or many. He may be Ithacan or Trojan. He may be English or Spanish, or a boy from Queens, New York. Texts place him in a thousand e-mails. Is he a human? Is he a song? Haven says,

> In song, men come pouring out
> Of horses they themselves have built.
> The living world, under the spell of
> song, opens its myriad-mouthed face
> and men like gods pour out.

But pour out of what? Song or earth? Haven still lives and therefore may yet choose.

The second fictional character is Thersites, a hunchbacked foot soldier. I first encountered him at a summer camp when I tried to read a prose translation of the *Iliad* by W. H. D. Rouse, because I thought reading such a book would make a man of me. I put him in my phantom sign.

> On the morning of Agamemnon's dream of victory
> Thersites wakes drenched with sleeplessness.
> Nights in camp were always the same:
> Toads and spiders and shrieking cicadas.
> But now Thersites can't believe his eyes.
> The army is splashing in the sea.
> It's here he utters the only sentence
> In twenty-four books I was sure I understood.

> "Let us all sail home," he cries,
> "And leave this man to digest his gorge of prizes."

Haven echoes Thersites.

> And his hunger
> pushes him
> to devour the light-
> filled openings he calls
> spaces. He sees emptiness;
> He is bodied yearning.

Thersites appears only once. After that, he slips back into nought. Did he die in battle? Did he make it home to Queens? Some say he was murdered by Achilles. No one knows. Of all the speakers in the *Iliad*, he is the only one unaccounted for.

He has no death.

Outside of horror books and Hamlet, it is rare for a character to make a debut after death, but Homer's third invention does just that. A sailor in the Ithacan crew, Elpenor gets drunk, falls off Circe's roof, and breaks his neck. "He shattered the nape nerve; the soul sought Avernus." His life was so inconsequential that when his shipmates sailed, he was left behind, like Mother at the rest stop. Only in the underworld did Odysseus encounter him, and ask

> "Elpenor, how did you come to this place,
> this gloomy darkness? You got here on foot
> faster than I did, sailing in my black ship."

Elpenor transmogrifies from supernumerary to magician who, by the agency of death, beats Odysseus to the underworld. Yet, there is also a hint of derision— "Ace, you were so slow on earth but you made it right quick into death." Still, on the verge of nought, Elpenor finally speaks.

Thersites and Elpenor. They did not live or die on earth. Their names shaped a poet's breath—if Homer breathed. But now their time has come. More than Achilles or Agamemnon or Odysseus, these figments of low birth and weak judgment reflect our modern world. They speak with mouths made wholly of text. Elpenor appears in Ezra Pound's Canto I.

> But first Elpenor came, our friend Elpenor,
> Unburied, cast on the wide earth,
> Limbs that we left in the house of Circe,
> Unwept, unwrapped in sepulchre, since toils urged other.
> Pitiful spirit.

And Thersites, who wailed from the boys' camp in my phantom sign, "Let us all be whole, be one, let us all sail home,"—he too has become multitudinously singular. Hegel coined "Thersitism." Nietzsche called him "Socrates's revenge." For Marx, he was a socialist hero. The great Cuban poet Roberto Manzano writes,

> consider well, Thersites, that everything's exhaustible,
> unsustainable,
>   weak, discardable, but has a perfect finish to it.

Yes, a perfect finish.

When Shakespeare wrote, "Thersites' body is as good as Ajax' / When neither are alive," did he realize Thersites never lived?

And Homer. He lives and does not live; he is Homeros and Numerous; Greek and Trojan and Brit and Basque and Yank. Even though they stride through Virgil, Dante, Pope, Tennyson, and Kazantzakis, only once has any Homeric hero escaped his shadow—and he needed a hex to do it—Leopold Bloom.

And our friend, Elpenor, unwept, unburied. I met him too, long ago. I did not hear Ezra channeling a ghost,

> "Ill fate and abundant wine. I slept in Circe's ingle.
> Going down the long ladder unguarded,
> I fell against the buttress,
> Shattered the nape-nerve, the soul sought Avernus."

I met Elpenor in the guise of another drunk falling off the roof of another epic.

In front of the hi-fi in Queens, I rocked to the sound of Elpenor's cracking skull, as Paddy and Tom and Liam and Tommy roared in full-throated vinyl

> One morning Tim got rather full
> His head felt heavy which made him shake,
> He fell from a ladder and he broke his skull
> And they carried him home his corpse to wake.

In the fall from Circe's ingle to Dublin pavement, Elpenor transmigrates into Finnegan.

> Mickey Maloney raised his head
> When a noggin o' whiskey flew at him.
> It missed him, fallin' on the bed.
> The liquor scattered over Tim.

Finnegan, Elpenor, Thersites—Homer rocked them into life. But who rocked Homer?

> Bedad you're alive! See how he rises.
> Timothy risin' from the bed,
> Says 'hurl your whiskey round like blazes,
> Thunder and lightnin' do you think I'm dead?"

The Muse, the Muse, the Muse. Plural singular; oneness in excess.

X

Every fourteen months, H. L. Hix delivers to me, his publisher, a manuscript. Since 2002, Etruscan has published twelve Hix titles, with two forthcoming. By itself, this output daunts, but Hix is the author of twenty-seven other books in five genres along with uncountable monographs, articles, and reviews. Tales of his graphomania are legion. Winter dawns, he dons Carhartt overalls to scrive in his Wyoming barn. Driving to class, he scribbles in a dashboard notebook. On his exercise bike, he memorizes sonnets.

"The formidable H. L. Hix," reviewers say. "The indefatigable Hix," making him sound like a British battleship. Once, when questioned about the fit of a thirty-page section of a manuscript regarding the Spanish Renaissance poet Fray Luis, Hix resubmitted, in eighteen days, a completely different sequence—this one in the voice of Jesus Christ—challenging the fecundity of the loaves and fishes.

The problem is that despite meticulous attention to prosody and unbridled originality, his prolificacy is often taken for verbosity. Such volume, readers think, must mean carelessness, if not self-indulgence. Even positive reviews sometimes begrudge. "Hix has a reputation," says one review, "for books conceived as projects, sometimes at the expense of individual poems. . . . Hix is at best stunningly inventive, at worst prolix." Another reviewer writes, "impressive enough as phrasemaker, as builder of forms, he shines when he has some reason to compress, to edit himself, to cut things down."

At a cocktail party, a pundit whispered in my ear, "I've finally drunk the Hix Kool-Aid," as if such labor spawned a cult. When I pitched a new Hix title to our distributor, a sales rep half-jokingly wondered if perhaps H. L. Hix and I weren't the same person, thus explaining why I publish these unsalable books. "Or maybe," he quipped, "there is more than one Hix."

"And why not," I wish I'd said. "After all, there are many Homers."

As Hix's publisher, I am not an Analyst. I am a Unitarian. There is just one Hix, I say, and it's up to me to get his name into the world. Even though the project of Hix studies is to question identity—blending voices, forms, styles, and even fonts to blur the notion of single authorship—I continue to print "H. L. Hix" on the front cover, racy blurbs on the back. "National Book Award Finalist" gets stamped on each new title. While Hix writes to erase, I strive to increase visibility. I want to make a brand of dissolution. Such is Universe City.

I could start a new marketing campaign, like the one my phantom sign did for Homer, where imaginary agents, editors, PR sharks, and marketers gather in a Queens shebeen to drool over the success of Homer's debut.

> The Iliad was a hit! (Who'd a thunk?)
> Burned down every kulcha market
> From Farrar Straus Giroux to Marvel Comics—
> Even Hollywood (check out the pecs
> On Brad).

And who's taking minutes but the bard himself.

> Item the first: Because the senior scriveners
> Have pressed upon yours truly the chore
> Of taking notes on all that happens here,
> I will at least amuse (revenge) myself
> In mock-heroic dudgeon as if
> I were Pope's Homer, or Homer's pope.
> (Forgive the self-aggrandizing trope).
> And if I break the meter, consider that
> Yesterday I learned the alphabet.

The Muse's plan, I'll call it. But Muse sounds portentous, antiquated as troubadour or rhapsode. Instead, I'll call my scheme X: named for an intangible entity meant to address another intangible entity: people.

X is the singular for plural energy.

In X, poetry does not respond to people, with their claims and hexes and hungers and eyeballs endlessly squinting poetry into prose. In X, poetry might flourish without people's knowledge or consent.

Our T-shirts read, "Got Nought?"

Our bumper stickers shout, "Verse is Universal."

"Stanzas," we tweet, "Understand."

Outside X, every perp gets the same dollop of personhood. Every Malthusian unit counts as one. In X, people=flesh+nought. The closer to absolute nought, the closer to X. Twenty-three hours, fifty-nine minutes, and nineteen seconds per day is the record, currently held by one Emmanuel D. McCluskey, a tantric swami last seen haunting particles and waves in Woodside, Queens. In X, nought can appear excessive.

Every marketing plan needs a story, and every story needs a hero. Hix is a tough sell. He is the least marketable of men. Ghostly pale, thin as a ricket, H. L. Hix sightings are rare as some endangered owl. He leads no cause, triggers no trauma, hallucinates no paradise. We could try a MacPherson con and conjure some Ossianic bard for him to channel. But that's a mug's game. Look what happened when some white dude named Mike Hudson tried to pass himself off as Yi-Fen Chou. To wax heroic, we'll have to remake Hix from the inside.

We'll call him Hxs. Scrabbling letters, Hxs is less singular, but not quite X. In X, Hxs has redacted everything ever written and incorporated all into one Hxsv opus with three purposes:

1. to reframe authorship, ownership, and identity
2. to bring the technology of the alphabet to bear on the fact that the alphabet is a technology—the first to which we are exposed, at so young an age that we see it not as a tool but as source of identity—bestowed in tablets or dreams by Thoth or Yahweh, certified by Homeric heroes Shaquille, Kobe, and LeBron who attest in public-service commercials that reading, as opposed to being gigantically athletic—is fundamental to happiness and success
3. to become X

Every story also needs a quest. So, let Hxs wend south through cornices plagiarized from Dante descending from human poet to murmuration of orchestrated voices. Imagine his skin dissolving to reveal the text beneath, flowing like *Matrix* data. Just before the final quench, Hxs encounters a human figure trudging up the path in the opposite direction—from plural into singular.

They halt. It's a cloudy midsummer day, though underground. Sky will be photoshopped. Hxs's body hums. The figure digs clay with his left foot.

"I come from Universe City," says Hxs.

"That's where I'm headed," says Homeros.

"I'm descending into Numerous," says Hxs.

"I'm climbing to be Homer," says Homeros.

"The mode of composition, the multiform, the traditional referentiality, the echoic resonance all belong to Numerous," Hxs says.

"The singularity, the omnivorous iconoclasm, the eclectic resonance, the Wyoming barn, are all attributed to Hix," says Homeros.

"Yet," allows Hxs, "it is equally impossible that you aren't Homer. Climbing down I have passed diverse pilgrims." Hxs thumbs backward up the tunnel. "Virgil, Dante, Tennyson, Kazantzakis, Pope—every cartoon Odysseus fingers Homer—only one Blooms out of reach."

"I don't know those guys," says Homeros. "I had only two comrades. I drew them as phantom signs that Homer was there, like Kilroy. Thersites is weak, Elpenor dumb.

"That's how I felt before the blank page," says Homeros.

"No page is blank," sighs Hxs.

"Every month I started weak and dumb," says Homeros, "waiting for the Muse, who had been always inside, rising from the limbus to the tongue . . . but now before the page I was alone—dumb and weak. I waited and waited as the moon swelled and brightened, the wind rose and stilled, and the sun clicked each morning over the sill of my office window and by the third week somehow the words were there on the page though I don't remember writing them. For a week I'd run around the room like a crazed beast. Then the chapter was finished and I was left alone at the start of the next month, weak and crippled as Thersites; dumb as Elpenor. Twenty-four times it happened. And that was the *Odyssey*. They don't know if I'm one or many? Neither do I."

"Analysts say," says Hxs, "Thersites and Elpenor evolved from the multiform as shadows of Achilles and Odysseus—stock figures meant simply to contrast. But I propose that after their embodiment by Pound and Joyce and Marx and Nietzsche and Manzano, we see them through a prism of refiguring and we imagine one Homeros, secretly working against the flow of Numerous, the way you secretly favored the Trojans over your Greek patrons. Beneath the text we see a single mind, composed of all the minds you spawned."

"Why are you bound for Numerous?" asks Homeros.

Hxs's fingers cross. "I want to become X," he says. "Poems are uncorrected proofs until they lose Hs. Written twice the same way a poem gives critics a target. Achilles and Odysseus are trapped in Greek. Thersites and Elpenor roam free, timeless."

"Thersites got beat down. Elpenor just fell off a roof," says Homeros.

"No," says Hxs, "Elpenor fell off the roof in an epic poem. Seeking Avernus, his soul found Ezra Pound. Clubbed by Odysseus, Thersites resurrected to speak for millions."

"My friends are heroes?" says Homeros. "Will I need to rewrite everything?"

"Everything's been done." Hxs waves a hand. "It's all a marketing scheme. What my publisher doesn't know is that I'm not coming back."

Homeros trudges upward toward Homer. "That's why I self-published," he mutters.

Finally, every story needs a dilemma. Mine is "how to stop Hix from working."

Ha! Good luck with that. Actually, my quandary is more difficult. I can't slow him, so I need to make Hix's work appear not to be work. As Yeats droned, back in the first chapter when we hardly knew each other, "A line will take us hours maybe" etc. Yeats understood that the reviews, the quips, the gossip, the buzz-kill, all reflect a zero-sum attitude. Only a given amount of authentic inspiration is allotted to each poet. Poetry can't look like work. Prose scribblers like Oates or Updike or King or Mailer don't suffer such criticism—or if they are tweaked, it's for repetition. Hix's poetry, according to reviewers, is "philosophically ambitious," "multiformed," "pithy," "kaleidoscopic." There is, simply, too much. Poetry, however original, cannot be trusted to the industry of human hands.

The more Hix manufactures, the less poetical he appears. When his Carhartts crouch over the plywood board and he peers through unpainted cracks at the endless winter dawn and skates his quill across foolscap, he is H. L. Hix. Not Homer or LeBron. Hix produces work. It is Hs. X is what we used to call the Muse.

Seeing poetry as a work product privileges intention over inspiration. Poetry becomes a closed system: people writing for people. Why mimic conventions of the vatic? Why spiral skyward into incoherence? Why imprecate? Why chant? Why rock? Why even rhyme? With no Muse to charm, why not just say what you mean?

Yeats feared work so much he played hooky with faeries and students from the Hermetic Order of the Golden Dawn and Madame Blavatsky and Communicators and Rosicrucians. For all the work of his "weary heart," Yeats spent most of his life peering forlornly through text to glimpse X.

He's not alone. All bookwrights eventually wind up "weary hearted." Sydney comes halting forth and Milton's sun is dark and Wordsworth would suckle pagans and Pound cannot make it cohere and Williams won't say what depends and Moore too dislikes it. We all long for a time when "lines were conceived and spoken in one breath."

The day my heart wearied, people shaved my chest and wheeled me into a room of processed light. X, they Mercurochromed. But nothing changed. Time ticked in again, moment by moment counted backward one by one, like sentences.

I never glimpsed cosmic scale. No earth-sized atom. Each breath reprised no poem. Was my life contained in nought? People had cut into my chest, held my heart in their hands, and replaced it. But returning from Avernus, I was dumb as Elpenor.

Thus I repented. I went back to work—da Da, da Da, da Da, da Da, da Da. From my heart's X, I made my phantom sign. Don't wobble, I told myself. Hold everything straight. Hold minutes, days, years, stanzas, books. Work has no Muse. The Muse is X.

Meanwhile, Hs vanished. Homeros clawed up all the way to Queens. Whether he was born or died, he lives. X marks his spot. One and one and one and never Numerous.

To the marketers, he says

> But I have not yet taken my turn.
> Items spiral and multiply. They wax
> Far past two hundred sixty-six
> As if recorded minutes stretched to eons.
> As if I exist on a white screen.
> As if I am not dead. Or never was.
> A rumor drifting through the subways.
>
> I know what they crave—the scriveners:
> Another sightless bust on a book cover.
> Some cheesy nostos, a sequel
> Featuring goodies cut from the original:
> The horse, the sack of Troy, Achilles's death,
> Ajax's suicide, Atrides's bloodbath.
> Monsters and sacred cows and magic wind,
> And an up-close-and-personal scoop on Helen.
>
> Let them indulge their epic fantasy.
> Rock on their thrones. Invoke the voice by proxy.
> My sequel is a memoir with no I's.
> My protagonist a perfect nobody.
> No dreamer like my hunchback Thersites.
> No One slaughters strife. Sacks theories.
> Harkens to no voice beside his own.
> He's farther than Ethiopia and immanent
> As the 5&10 on Northern and Main.
>
> To scriveners his madness will seem feigned.
> But when they come to take him from his island,
> He'll place his son before the veering plough
> And slice the cord that binds him to the world.

;

is the sign of the foot; ball and heel earthbound; sole arching skyward like a shell. Except for the face, the foot is the most recognizable human feature; it articulates intelligence and will. I could not tell friends by nipple or elbow or knee or ear or even hand; I know their foot.

The sea nymph's foot was noble and expressive. The pointer was slightly longer than the hallux, a yellowish quarter moon crowning the heel. There was inland light between each toe. The nails glowed with unvarnished sheen. When she glided by, there was an nth of air between sole and rug.

Tall, I could no longer kiss my foot. I became an unpent ouroboros.

From utterance to page, Homer dropped a foot. The flex, the curl, the stretch, the spread, and elegance could not be rendered justly in two dimensions. But he gained the sign.

; looks archaic when sentenced, like nought. But naked, ; is gay; it does not heed what comes before or after; it is the gash through which the hex gushes out of darkness; it is two separate marks strangely paired.

; is the sign of the foot: dependent and free; leaping and in step; in air and on land. Something there is absurd about the foot, like poet; it is rude and complex; it is trouty; its tributary bones are myriad; it is susceptible of rings and corns; its condition speaks to injustice. Zairians played basketball barefoot; Air Jordans sustain a global industry. Women suffer binding; suffer heels; Cinderella is illustrative.

; speaks to the sole; it is both toe and heel. Revelation comes only with repose. ; is the wobble in the gait. It is the pebble and Achilles's heel.

In the time of the sea nymph, I sat down at the foot of Yeats. His glittering eyes were gay, but his sock was rent, the hole redressed with black India ink. Because I had rocked on hands and knees for years I knew the Sidhe and Fergus and Knocknarea and who hadn't eaten Parnell's heart. But this was Universe City, a land of Escher cubicles and Harris Tweed and study cliques and stiletto ripostes. The men were peaty and doe-eyed; the women staunch and unadorned. Of gyres or Noh or Kenner I knew nought. I did not know why everyone was ponderous or why rhyme displeased; I did not know if I could master the thing most prized in Universe City: Meaning.

"What does it mean?" asked no one ever, because they knew and could explicate at length. Tall did not count. I did not know who (if anyone) hunched around the seminar lamp would hex me; I did not know if I had sufficient mind or how the epic with the sea nymph would resolve. I did not know how this travail would shape a future. Yeats was gay; he knew nought and all.

The bear at the head of the oak slab seldom spoke; with each explication or quip his fur riffled; on occasion he released a grunt or sigh. We cubs slouched under the mantle of marble busts: Keats, Wordsworth, Milton, Tennyson, Pope. The bear snarled at Milton and cuffed Tennyson. We waited our turn to stand on hind legs. We did not heed whoever played lead cub; we did not deign to note. We cocked our heads. We bit pencils. We jiggled knees. We hoped, vaguely, that this week's cub's hair would go up in flames or the chair under his or her bony ass crashed through the floor.

The night came when the bear's paw swiped at me. It was "Easter, 1916." I looked down at my foot. Long ago in front of the hi-fi I had rocked to the poem in the sonorous voice of Tom Clancy. I knew utterance, but not sign. I did not know that ; is the sole through which Yeats stepped from Queens to Universe City.

The bear if you must know is Galway Kinnell. There are no ; in Kinnell. His poems are utterance. His foot was claw-splayed. That night to ground myself I held in my mind the sea nymph's divine sole against my cock.

"I have met them at close of day coming with vivid faces."

Head tilted, rocking slightly, I chanted. I did not know lines; I had never seen the poem. When I came to "Eighteenth century houses" I tried to tamp the Clancy down my throat. I shoved "houses" forward in the palate; the tongue fluted "passed" to Queens "paas." It was hard to speak like me. Clancy had shaped the air inside my mouth.

The fiddle rose and hovered on "beauty is born."

The circle of cubs sniffed the air and tensed.

"Read straight," their eyebrows said. "Don't plagiarize a brogue."

The bear's eyes jaundiced. He chewed on the ear of the cub sitting beside him.

Next came two stanzas Clancy had left out.

In lines now, in Queens English, I explicated: Padraic Pearse "rode our wingèd horse." "That woman's days were spent in ignorant good-will" by Countess Markievicz; Thomas MacDonagh, "coming into his force," translated Cathal buí Mac Giolla Ghunna's "An Bannán Buí"; Major John MacBride of Boer fame "had done most bitter wrong" to Maud Gonne, Yeats's sea nymph.

This was Universe City; Yeats and Homer were subjects; MacDonagh and MacBride and Connolly and Pearse were in the poem and outside the lines in history, like Odysseus and Achilles.

And true it was that I saw on the page what I had never heard. The rhymes unschemed—cloud and road; stream and brim; the chant descended into common speech.

> The horse that comes from the road;
> The rider, the birds that range
> From cloud to tumbling cloud,
> Minute by minute they change;

Horse and rider and birds and cloud changed into lines. It was not nature but some skein of nature: Noh, or Lapis Lazuli, or Lissadell, or romantic Ireland, dead and gone—mirror on mirror mirrored was all the show.

> A shadow of cloud on the stream
> Changes minute by minute;
> A horse-hoof slides on the brim,
> And a horse plashes within it;

Was it possible to know both cloud and hoof? To be present with the bear and the busts and Yeats and the foot of the sea nymph and at the same time be the boy in Queens at the hi-fi rocking and chanting—backward washed clean of birth; forward into days charted by lines; backward like a wave or a half rhyme; and forward into "Easter, 1916," when I first bent solemn to the page?

In Universe City, "long-legged moor-hens dive" and do not dive, and "hens to moor-cocks call" and do not call. "Minute by minute they live" and do not live. By sitting still and bolting eyes to the page and reading mouth closed and following nought but meaning, could I not do both?

Or is my whole life from the days of sea nymph to my throne as desiccated professor in faraway Youngstown, Ohio, one hundred years after 1916 "needless death after all"? I am older than Yeats in Easter; older than the bear. My heart troubles the living stream; it has been surgically bypassed to a stone.

In the final stanza Clancy powers forth and the fiddle flourishes, but in the seminar room my eyes focused, and although it may be "Our part to murmur name upon name" that night the murmuring was soundless.

Then I came to the vortex of utterance and sign.

> We know their dream; enough
> To know they dreamed and are dead.

; is the sign of the foot. Touching the phantom foot of the sea nymph, I felt the sole. "Enough" was sole; set apart from the bodhrán's double spondee by ;, on the edge of the page aching to be born.

"Dream;" is the only ; in the poem that troubles the living line.
Had Yeats writ only the heel, the dream would die:

> We know they dreamed, [only well] enough
> To know they dreamed and are dead,

Had he used only the toe—

> We know they dreamed. [It is]Enough
> To know they dreamed and are dead,

the dream would drown the world.

Without descending into speech, the bear said, "'Poems Against the Alphabet' is our course. The curriculum is 'Utterance over Sign.'"
The bear cubs scrambled for pencils and notepads.
The bear growled that all of us were Yeats.
"Poem," he bellowed, "is the agent of metempsychosis."
"Heed no X," he commanded. "O is enough to know."
His paws climbed the air. "Not just Yeats," he roared.
The cubs scurried under the table.
"Homer, too, before he fell to signs. The first words of the first poem were not addressed to people.
"Sing, Goddess," he sang. And the bear sat.

But the poem had not ended. Clancy chanted. Yeats still spun. Huddled with the cubs under the table I heard "excess of love bewildered them." Even though he had lost the sea nymph, Yeats did not want to die a needless death. But the curve of the foot pulled him; the chthonic print impelled; it was not the men themselves—not Padraic Pearse and James Connolly and Thomas MacDonagh and John MacBride—no, it was not then and is not now the men; it is the transposition of their names into XS.

> MacDonagh and MacBride
> And Connolly and Pearse.

The cadence reaches crescendo; the fiddle wails.
; is the sign of the gulf between rocking in front of the hi-fi and sitting at my desk a century after Easter, 1916. It is the phantom foot.

"I write it out in a verse," writes Yeats.

"Begin anywhere you will," writes Homer.

; is the sign of the foot. The toe holds fast; the heel digs the vortex of the gyre.

I write ; out in a verse in Universe City, where I live.

O

Before the alphabet, there were phantom signs. In clouds, in twilit branches, in bird entrails. Every nightmare spawned a tusk, a wooden horse, a treetop bed. But who could read?

At the opening O of utterance stood a phantom X.

X is nobody's birth sign. Where lab coats unscrewed my heart and ticked it back in place, X was the sign they made.

One breath and O dissolved.

O *please*. Dissolve is not my hex. I pulsed, thrust, kicked, slid, trudged.

As I X'd utterance to sign, every chapter mewled weak and dumb, as the moon swelled and wind rose and the sun beat and by midnight Xs scarred the scroll. Like a crazed beast I galloped through the night, then collapsed. Next month I began again weak as Thersites, dumb as Elpenor. The foot kept spasm-time; arms hugged the scar; the earth strained to hold the stallion eye.

Though my phantom sign has gestated to codex, titled *To Banquet with the Ethiopians,* with ISBN and blurbs and acid-free, dust-jacketed cloth, few read. It has produced insufficient stars to grind the algorithm. Book clubs abstain. Libraries demur. Big boxes boomerang returns.

Therefore, my phantom sign may yet be capable of change. It may be nought inside the haven of gay hex.

To my publisher I say, "Larry, old chum, Homer was remaindered until foreign sales kicked in."

When Universe City took Homer's breath away, lines were no longer conceived and spoken in one breath. The *Iliad* was TXT. O Xed out. Nine years of war condensed to twenty-three hours of nought and the tenth folded to fifty days. Troy burned like paper. The cosmos cooled to an escutcheon and

> . . . heavens, earth, sea, the untiring sun,
> Cities of mortal men, dancers whirling,
> Shepherds, farmland, vineyards, sheaves of wheat—
> Every harmonious note the child had sung—

And even the sleek foot of Strife herself,
All hardened to gleaming bronze tableaus
Forged by a lame god for a killer's shield.

Universe City is a bronze tableau.

In my mind's tableau, the sea nymph whispered that Numerous was Homeros then Homer.

"Book Six," she said, and I heard Sex.

"Nested in the scroll," sang the sea nymph, and I imagined us nested under gossamer sheets, "stitched into the weave of blood and war, Homeros first glimpsed it. He did not know its name. It was everything and nothing. It held his gaze. He could no longer hear cadence or see panoply; there was no smoke or towers or shields or chariot; yet it cleaved open each mind—warriors and kings and common grunts. It stretched from toe to heel of every line and story. It yielded his own beginning and his end in a distant land. He drew a line across."

The sea nymph's phantom finger traced my future scar.

"And then another." She crossed the phantom trace.

"He called it X," she surged into my old age.

"Inscribing X," the sea nymph tongued my ear from far away, "Homeros lost O.

"He was Homer. Had always been, but never so alone. Deep in X, he felt stillness at the vortex of time's surge. X was his sole companion and confidant. And thus he whispered himself into text."

The sea nymph rocked back and forth through time chanting as Homer.

"'From the vast forest of blood and pain and death I rock with my eyes closed and pick one tiny leaf.

"'Glaucus, I name it. Brightness.

"'I call it grandson of Bellerophon. I strip its armor. I deliver helmet and hauberk to its enemy. In the flame and smoke of battle no one will see. Here in this bright leaf I plant my X. Glaucus will say

"Generations of men are like the leaves
In winter, wind blows them down to earth,
But then, when spring season comes again,
The budding wood grows more. And so with men.
One generation grows, another dies away."

"'But no one sees I have inscribed the opposite, as no one saw I secretly loved my secretly native Troy.

"'Generations never pass; winds are motionless, and budding wood stays forever young. In X, everything is always as it was.'"

So sang the nymph as Homer in my ear.

When she regained her form, she yawned and stretched. Across the ages she looked at me and said, "Behind Glaucus's utterance is written speech—a sign that Homeros had always been Homer, even when rocking and chanting."

The sea nymph rocked and chanted in forever now.

"The sign," she whispered into generations, "was Fearless Bellerophon."

Bellerophon hexed Fearless is my sign.

My class notes tell the story of Book Six. "The queen wanted Fearless Bellerophon, but he would not sleep with her, so the queen whispered a story to the king. The king was furious, but would not murder Bellerophon, his guest. Instead, the king sent Bellerophon to a far country, carrying a phantom sign, inscribed on a folded sheaf."

Bellerophon, first publisher, delivered, but did not die.

It was the night the sea nymph vanished from our bed without a sign.

What was the queen's tale?

What was the king's sign no one could read?

Am I making up a story of spurned love?

Am I inscribing signs no one can read?

"Nought," says the bear, waving a paw.

"23 hours," says Hix, still undissolved.

";" says Yeats, stepping into dream.

"What a dashing man," says nobody, ever.

There is no reader but there is a sign. What is not in Bellerophon's tableau? It contains *A Heaven Wrought of Iron* and *The Avenue Bearing the Initial of Christ into the New World* and *Saint Judas* and *Rain Inscription* and *Heart's Needle* and "Easter, 1916" and *To Banquet with the Ethiopians: A Memoir of Life Before the Alphabet.*

In Bellerophon's tableau

> . . . warriors strive and gods fix their gaze,
> And millennia of scriveners make their bones.
> And nothing can ever change or be forgotten.

Bellerophon's tableau contains every X that breaks, and every O that's heals, and every wave of silence yet to come.